PAINT IT!

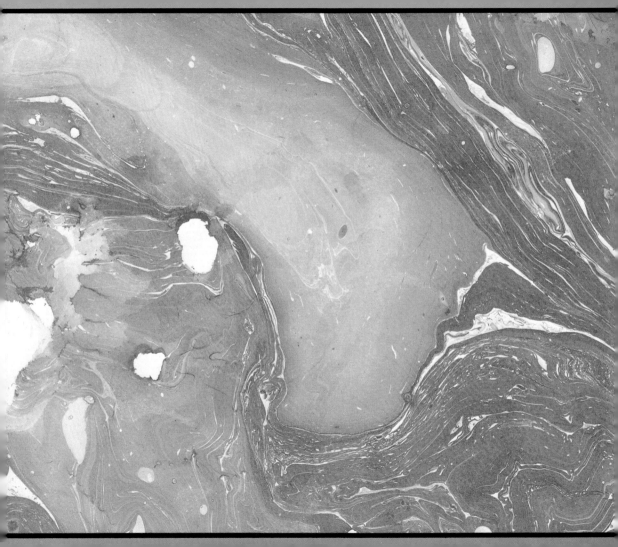

PAINT IT!

HOW TO DECORATE FABRIC, CHINA & GLASS

·J·U·L·I·E·T· ·B·A·W·D·E·N·

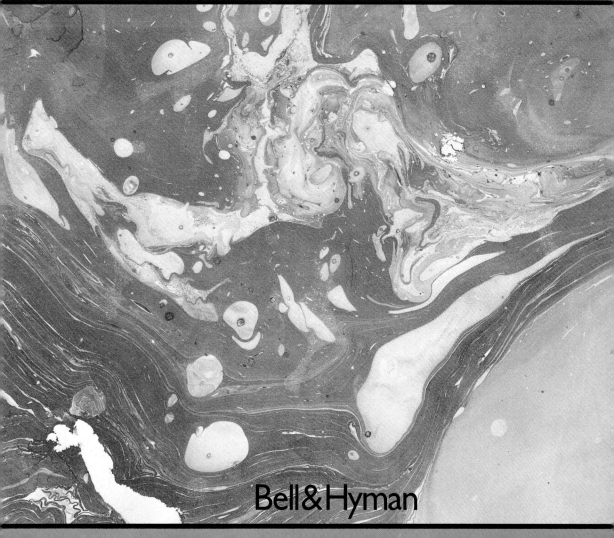

Bell & Hyman

For my parents Anthony Oates Bawden and Berjouhie Bawden with love.

First published 1986 by Bell & Hyman Limited
Denmark House
37-39 Queen Elizabeth Street
London SE1 2QB
© Juliet Bawden 1986

Photography by Greg Hunter

Designed by John Grain
Artwork by Hilary Evans
Typeset by Typecast Ltd., East Peckham, Tonbridge
Printed and bound in Portugal by Printer Portuguesa, Sintra

ISBN 0 7135 2707 2

British Library Cataloguing in Publication Data

Bawden, Juliet
Paint it!
1. Decoration and ornament
I. Title
745.7'2   NK1510

CONTENTS

ACKNOWLEDGEMENTS

The author and publishers wish to thank the following people and organizations for their generous help: Artemis Products Ltd, who supplied the range of Pebeo paints, dyes and brushes used throughout the book, with particular thanks to Susan Fairbairn Cole for her help and technical advice and for supplying the finished objects on pp.7, 58 top right, 62, 63 top right and top left, 66 and 67 the last 5 projects are based on designs by Dover Publicatons Inc; Acorn Fabrics, who supplied the silk used for the silk paintings; Arding and Hobbs for lending the chairs for the photograph on page 78; G.P. & J. Baker Ltd. who supplied all the furnishing and curtain fabric used; the manufacturers Brother and Jones for the use of the 'Compal Galaxie' electronic sewing machine, used to make all the sewn items in the book; David Constable of Candle Makers Supplies; Dorma who supplied the duvet cover; special thanks to Dagny Duckett who painted the items on pp. 74, 75 and 122; Greg Hunter for taking the photographs; Helen Pask; Sunway who supplied the blinds; Tootal Craft Ltd who supplied the thread and notions used for making the cushions, curtains and deckchair covers. Thanks also to Mike, Jack, Oliver and Wendy who put up with my working long hours and covering every available surface in paint!

Silk painting

INTRODUCTION

This book shows you how to add individual touches to your home without necessarily spending lots of time or money. It contains ideas for painting on ceramics, fabrics, glass, metal, walls and wooden objects. Most of the projects are quick to carry out, and are finished in a few hours. None needs expensive equipment or involves complicated methods of application.

The paints used have been developed with both domestic and professional consumers in mind. The resulting products do not need complicated fixing or setting procedures to finish them, and result in the finest quality and colours.

I have used Pebeo paints throughout the book, but most of the projects are equally possible using other products designed for the same job — consult the manufacturer's instructions before you begin.

If you would like to paint a mural, a blind or some crockery but are not sure how to go about it, read on. You do not have to be very artistic or talented — just follow the instructions and have a go! I hope that you will have as much fun painting the designs as I have had, and that you will go on to develop your own designs and ideas.

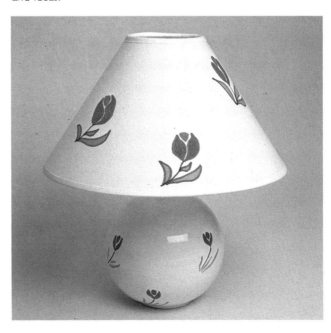

White Tulip lampshade

DESIGN SOURCES

Most designers do not wait for design inspiration before starting a project — they work at it. Very little is completely new in design, and most ideas are developed from a source, often bearing little obvious relation to the finished product. Rough sketches of animals, insects and flowers, or of sculptures and paintings in museums and galleries can form the basis of varied designs and motifs in ceramics, fashion and graphics.

You'll see this clearly in this book. Different pieces of fruit, a cup and saucer, a cat and its paw prints, and even simple wavy lines similar to those drawn by children learning to write have all provided the basis for unusual ideas for decorating objects. I hope that you will feel confident enough to adapt the projects to your taste, to change the motifs between different projects and to search for your own patterns and sources around you — look at brickwork, stained glass windows, magazines, market places . . . the list is endless.

TO CONVERT VISUAL INFORMATION INTO DESIGNS

Here are some quick, easy and fun methods of achieving some professional results without being a great artist. Take a vase of flowers:

1. It can be drawn, painted or photographed.
2. The photo can be a print, or a slide. The slide may be projected on to a wall or piece of furniture and the shapes drawn round as a preliminary to painting a mural.
3. You can project on to squared paper for a tapestry design to be woven or sewn in needlepoint.
4. The design can be simplifed, and stylized to form a pattern for a stencil design.
5. You can trace off the photo or drawing and make a mirror image of the design.
6. The drawing can be simplifed, elongated and used as a border design.
7. Designs can be squared up or down, thus changing the scale of the design:

To square up a design: Draw a square grid either on an existing drawing or on a piece of tracing paper which fits over the drawing.

To enlarge or decrease: Either copy the drawing onto dressmaker's grid paper or draw your own grid. You can of course draw a grid directly onto the object on which you wish to draw or paint.

Transferring the design: Transfer the design from the original one square at a time, making sure that lines and motifs appear in the same place in a large square as they did in a small one.

8. Photocopiers can be used to copy a photograph or drawing, to increase or decrease the size of the image you are using.

CERAMIC PAINTS

Painting ceramics is great fun and by the use of some of the techniques given, you can achieve professional results easily without having to be a great artist. To start with you should only work on glazed ceramics — you can then 'rub out' any mistakes with white spirit before the paint dries.

I used a range of solvent-based air-drying ceramic paints called Ceramic à Froid by Pebeo. Rather than fixing these in an oven or kiln, you just leave them to dry for at least 24 hours. Other manufacturers produce similar paints, which could equally well be used for most of the projects in this chapter, but do not use water-based paints in conjunction with white spirit. Take care, as always, to read the manufacturer's instructions before starting work. Do not mix water-based paints with solvent-based ones.

Pebeo's range of 22 opaque ceramic colours including gold, silver and pearl, can be further extended by mixing different shades. For a semi-opaque finish you can mix Ceramic à Froid paints with Couleurs Vitrails, transparent stained glass paints. In this chapter the paints listed for each project are ceramic paints unless otherwise stated.

Ceramic paints, though durable, are best used decoratively rather than for objects which come in for heavy wear. You should never put painted objects into a dishwasher. Gentle hand washing, or cleaning with white spirit is best. Plates need to be handled with special care since the design sits on top of the plate. You will have to take care not to scratch it with a knife and fork. Mugs, cups and saucers, and other items can clearly be used — otherwise there would be little point in painting them! (Items decorated with an all-over paint cover can be further protected with clear varnish.)

BEGINNERS' TIPS

1. Before you start, always have plenty of greaseproof paper or newspaper around on which to place the finished articles.
2. Always make sure the item to be painted is clean and free of grease. Wash it in warm, soapy water or clean it with white spirit before you begin.

3. Wear rubber gloves when spraying, sponging or marbling as this paint is not easily removed from the skin. You can buy fine gloves such as those used by hairdressers. Alternatively use a barrier cream on your hands. If you do get paint marks on your skin, use white spirit to remove them.

4. Make sure you have sufficient white spirit to wash brushes and dilute the paint. You will also need jam jars and lids or saucers for mixing paints.

5. Keep at least two soft, non-fluffy cloths beside you. One should be dipped in white spirit to wipe off mistakes, the other kept dry to wipe off any smear left by the wet one.

6. Never overload your brush with paint, unless you want to drip blobs of paint onto the object as part of the pattern.

7. Choose a selection of paint brushes ranging from fine to thick. These come in standard sizes and I give the brush number for each project. I used Pebeo brushes throughout. Buy the best brushes that you can afford as these keep their shape if properly looked after. Always wash them out thoroughly immediately they are finished with, and stand them in a jar with the handle facing down and the brush on top. If possible, have different brushes for water-based and solvent-based paints and store separately.

USEFUL EQUIPMENT

Sponge
Use small pieces of natural sponge for sponging on the paint.

Chinagraph pencil
Draw your design onto ceramic with this wax pencil. You can also use it as a resist (see Basic Techniques p.112).

Bowl
A large washing up bowl filled with water is used to float solvent-based ceramic or glass paint for marbling.

Mouth diffusing spray
This consists of two pieces of metal tube hinged together with a mouthpiece on the end of one piece. The bottom of the longer

piece of the tube is dipped in the colour you wish to spray. The gap at the elbow of the diffuser is pointed to where you wish to spray and you blow through the mouthpiece. This causes thousands of tiny particles of paint to fly out and land on the object in a fine and even coating.

Masking tape
Use this to mask off areas you don't want painted, creating a quick form of stencil. Be sure to flatten the edges with the back of a spoon handle to prevent seepage and wait at least 24 hours until the paint is absolutely dry before you remove the tape.

Low tack soft peel masking film
Ideal for making stencils for use on surfaces which aren't flat such as plates, cups, and saucers when conventional stencils would be cumbersome. A sharp knife or scalpel is needed to cut the stencil. Use it very gently and lift out the cut away areas. Peel off the adhesive backing very gently.

Old toothbrush
Use this for flicking paint to get a slightly heavier result than you do with a diffuser. Dip the brush in paint and then use a knife to pull the bristles back and release the paint onto the surface you wish to cover.

Stencil knife
For cutting stencils and paper.

Stencil paper

Stencil brush (es)

White spirit
To clean your brushes.

ZEBRA-STRIPED PLATE

Simplifed and stylized animals appear in children's books and on greetings cards and their markings can be transferred on fabrics and ceramics — look in the design dictionary at the back of the book for animal markings and footprints.

Method

1. Outline the zebra stripes on the plate, either in pencil or with a fine line of black paint.
2. Fill in the centres of the stripes with even strokes of black paint.
3. When dry, give a further coat of paint if the result is uneven.

Materials

Black ceramic paint
Brush no. 3
A white plate

Below: Sunrise Plate.

Below: Flan Dish.

SUNRISE PLATE

This plate is based on an old radio design. The design is drawn on p. 13 (below left).

Method

1. Trace or copy the design in outline.
2. Fill in the black stripes with even strokes of the brush.

Materials

Black ceramic paint
Brush no. 3
White plate

DOTS AND DASHES PLATE

Use self-adhesive shapes from stationers', either as they are, or cut into other shapes such as semi-circles and crescents, triangles, stripes and diamonds.

Method

1. Stick the shapes randomly or in an even pattern all over the plate. Press them down firmly to prevent paint from seeping under them.
2. Cover the rest of the plate in an even coat of black paint and leave to dry for at least 24 hours until the paint is completely dry.
3. Remove the sticky shapes.
4. At this stage you can paint on another colour, or add more stickers to build up different colours and shapes.

Materials

*Self-adhesive squares
and circles
Black ceramic paint
Brush no. 6
A white plate*

RIPPED MASKING TAPE DESIGN

Method

1. Rip the tape in half lengthways.
2. Stick the tape on the plate very firmly, placing the neat edges back to back to create two jagged edges.
3. Paint the areas not covered by the tape.
4. Allow to dry before removing the tape.
5. Alternatively, stick unconnecting pieces of tape down and paint the remaining areas.
6. Or paint one colour and allow to dry. Remove and stick tape down in a different position. Paint new areas another colour. Start with the lighter colours and build up gradually to the darker ones.

Materials

*Black ceramic paint
Masking tape
A white plate
Brush no. 6*

FLAN DISH

Method

1. Trace or copy the design on p. 13 (below right).
2. Fill in the black areas evenly with a brush.
3. N.B. This flan dish should not be used for oven baking after it has been decorated.

Materials

Black ceramic paint
Brush no. 2
White flan dish

BLUE AND GOLD PLATE

Method

1. Dip the dry sponge into the blue paint. Starting in the centre of the plate and working outwards, cover the plate in blue. Apply the paint by moving the sponge in small circular movements as though washing up. Keep the colour in the centre dense and thin it out towards the edge.
2. Load brush with white paint and drip into centre of plate.
3. Clean brush thoroughly with white spirit and repeat step 2 with gold paint.

Materials

CERAMIC PAINTS:
Sevres blue
Gold
White
Dry sponge
Brush no. 3
A white plate
Gloves

TADPOLES

This design is a combination of sponging and painting.

Method

1. Thin the lavender paint with a little white spirit.
2. Dip the sponge in the mixture, and sponge onto the plate leaving fairly large gaps between sponge marks. Leave until it is either tacky or dry.
3. Overload the paint brush with green and paint tadpole shapes on the plate. This is done by making the point where the paint brush touches the plate into the head of the tadpole and then painting a wiggly line from the head.

Materials

A white plate
Lavender ceramic paint
Victoria Green ceramic paint
Brush no. 3
Small square of sponge
White spirit

FRIED EGG PLATE

A fried egg is part of the design on this plate.

Method

1. Paint an egg shape in white.
2. Paint the yolk in yellow.
3. Using a brush no. 2 paint a slight blue shadow round part of the edge of the yolk. Brush it into the yellow so there is no hard line.
4. Make the pattern on the plate. Using orange paint and a brush no. 3 paint squiggles around the egg.
5. With a brush no. 2 paint blue zig zags between the orange squiggles.
6. Paint pinhead dots using Sevres blue on the orange squiggles.
7. Paint a white fleck or large sideways comma in white on the egg yolk.

Materials

A white plate
CERAMIC PAINTS:
White
Rich Yellow
Sevres Blue
Orange
BRUSHES
Nos. 2 and 3

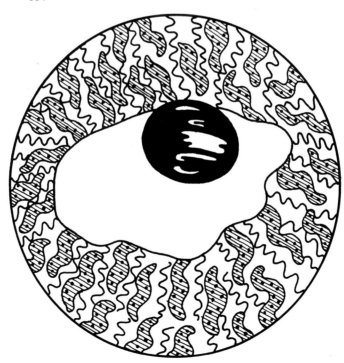

Opposite: Blue and Gold Plate.

Left: Tadpoles.

Below: Fried Egg Plate.

BLUE AND GOLD CUP AND SAUCER

The cup and saucer were treated in the same way as the pale glazed plate, and then a second colour was added.

Method

1. Dilute blue paint with white spirit and follow steps 1-3 for Pale Glazed Plate on p.24. Leave until tacky — approximately 3 hours.
2. Pour some gold paint into a saucer.
3. Scrunch up a handful of newspaper and dip it in the gold paint.
4. Pat any surplus paint onto spare paper, and then pat the gold paint onto the cup and saucer. Leave to dry.

Materials

Sevres blue ceramic paint
White spirit
Sponge
Gold ceramic paint
Gloves
Newspaper
Cup and saucer

CROCODILE PLATE

Method

1. Copy outline from the drawing opposite onto plate, copying the head and body separately if you wish to change the angle of the head.
2. Mix black and white paints together to make a dark grey.
3. Using a brush no. 2 with very little paint on it, paint over the outline of the crocodile in grey, rubbing out any mistakes with a cloth soaked in white spirit.
4. When you are satisfied with the outline, paint on the eye and the markings, which are just a series of half circles. Leave until tacky.
5. Mix a minute amount of grey with some Victoria green and colour in the top half of the crocodile with the brush no. 3.
6. Mix some white into the green mixture you have just used and colour in the lower half of the crocodile with the brush no. 3.
7. Paint a fly within eye view of the crocodile, using black paint and the brush no. 2.

Materials

CERAMIC PAINTS:
black
white
Victoria green
BRUSHES:
Nos. 2 and 3
A white plate
White spirit

MARBLED CUP AND SAUCER

It is much easier to cover a flat or convex object when marbling than it is a concave one. This is because water will fill up a bowl or saucer and the paint will float on the water rather than sticking to the surface, whereas on a flat or convex object the water will drip off.

Method

1. Dilute the blue paint with white spirit on one saucer.
2. Dilute the mauve with white spirit on another.
3. Pour the mixture onto water in a washing up bowl and mix it gently around, either by stirring with the back of a paint brush or pencil, or by blowing on the surface of the water.
4. Lay the saucer carefully on the surface of the water so that the paint sticks to it, gently remove from the water.
5. Repeat with the cup.
6. You can also use undiluted paint, in which case only a few drops are needed.

Materials

Sevres blue ceramic paint
White spirit
Mauve ceramic paint
Washing up bowl, glass bowl, or kitchen sink
Old paint brush (any size) or a pencil, for stirring
Cup and saucer

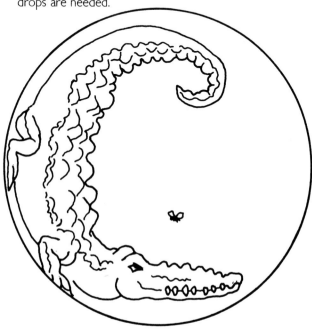

Crocodile Plate.

Opposite: Blue and Gold Cup and Saucer.

Left: Marbled Cup and Saucer.

Below: Crocodile Plate.

PALE GLAZED PLATE

Method	Materials
1. Dilute some paint with a little white spirit until it is the consistency of milk.	*Lavender ceramic paint*
2. Load the sponge with the mixture and dab it onto the plate until it is completely covered.	*White spirit* *Sponge (natural)* *A white plate*
3. Leave to dry. Don't worry if the paint runs down the plate in rivulets — this is part of the pattern. Try not to move the plate while it is drying.	*Gloves*

SPRAYED GOLD AND PINK PLATE

Method	Materials
1. Put a mixture of gold paint and thinners in the diffuser and spray the plate (see page 11).	*Gold ceramic paint* *Cyclamen pink ceramic paint*
2. When dry, respray using a mixture of cyclamen and white spirit in the diffuser.	*White spirit* *Diffuser* *Thinners* *A white plate* *Gloves*

WILDLIFE CUPS AND SAUCERS

Method

1. Trace the outlines from the templates onto the cups.
2. Colour in figures in appropriate colours, waiting for the first colour to dry before applying others.
3. For variations think of other animals and prints: rabbits, teddy bears, frogs, footprints, or even a pair of red wellies. Some ideas are listed in the design dictionary, but why not think up your own?

Materials

CERAMIC PAINTS:
DUCKS:
rich yellow
lavender
turquoise
black
CAT:
red
brown
PHEASANT:
brown
blue
yellow
Brush no. 3
Cups and saucers

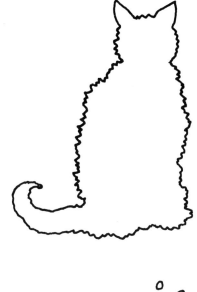

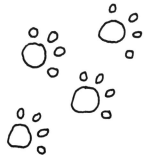

Overleaf:
Left Above: Plate Glazed Plate and Sprayed Gold and Pink Plate.

Left Below: Wildlife Cups and Saucers.

Right: Hand Painted Vase.

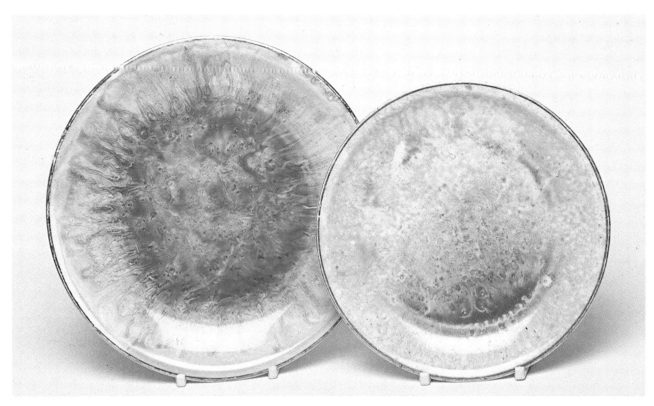

HAND PAINTED VASE IN BLACK AND GOLD

The design of this vase is inspired by lino print and wood cut motifs.

Method

1. Paint the zig zag outlines freehand, as you did when you were learning to write at school.
2. If you have an icing turntable or a tin or box to stand the pot on whilst painting, you can turn it round to see the vase as a whole.
3. Vary the texture of the paint as you fill in the shapes. Some parts are painted with very wet paint, and on other sections the paint is dry enough to show the brush strokes. Build up you own design of different dots, blobs, lines and patterns.
4. Add the further gold embellishment once the black paint is dry.

Materials

Black ceramic paint
Gold ceramic paint
Brush no. 4
Flower vase

TULIP PLATE

A very simple yet stylish design.

Method

1. Trace design onto plate.
2. Paint tulip heads in cherry red. Leave until tacky.
3. Paint in the leaves in Victoria green.

Materials

Cherry red ceramic paint
Victoria green ceramic paint
Brush no. 3
White plate

FISH DISH

Method

1. Outline the fish in black. Leave to dry.
2. Add splashes of colour in glass paint to give the translucent effect.

Materials

Black ceramic paint
Chartreuse green transparent glass paint
Turquoise glass paint
Brush no. 2
Small dish

Opposite: Tulip Plate.

Fish Dish.

TULIPS IN A VASE

A very brightly coloured plate with a lot of life.

Method

1. Trace the design onto the plate.
2. Paint the base in purple, leaving two blank squares in it, which will later be painted yellow, as in the photograph.
3. Paint a wavy line the width of the paint brush in yellow above the purple.
4. Paint a broad wavy line of orange above the yellow and another fine line of yellow above the orange.
5. Paint the leaves and stalks in a mixture of Victoria green and emerald.
6. Paint blobs of cherry red on top of the stalks to form the heads of the tulips.
7. Paint turquoise lines randomly over the plate.

Materials

CERAMIC PAINTS:
mauve
rich yellow
orange
Victoria green
emerald
cherry red
turquoise
black
Brush no. 3
White plate

8. Draw a line of red 1cm (½in) up from the base of the vase and colour underneath this line to the edge of the plate.
9. Paint the two blank squares on the vase with yellow.
10. Paint black dots randomly all over the plate, including the vase.

FLORAL PLATE ON GREEN BACKGROUND

Method

1. Paint free-flowing flowers in red, mauve and white, following the rough design. Leave until tacky.
2. Fill in the centre with black blobs.
3. Paint the background with Victoria green.

Materials

CERAMIC PAINTS:
red
mauve
white
black
Victoria green
Brush no. 3
White plate

Left: Daffodil Plate.

Right: Floral Plate.

PLATE USING A RESIST METHOD

The resist method in painting involves covering part of the object you are going to decorate with a substance which will not allow the paint to penetrate it. Chinagraph pencil will resist ceramic and glass paints. The finished effect will be that the covered areas will retain the background colour while the other areas will accept the newly applied paint.

Method

1. Draw the outline of the design on the plate with the chinagraph.
2. Fill in those leaves you want to remain white with the chinagraph.
3. Fill in the flower shapes with turquoise and pink.
4. Paint the background mauve.
5. Leave to dry and harden for at least 24 hours.
6. Dip a paint brush into white spirit and paint over the chinagraph markings. These will dissolve and leave areas and outlines in white.

Materials

Chinagraph pencil
CERAMIC PAINTS:
turquoise
pink
mauve
Brush no. 3
White spirit
White plate

Left: Plate using a resist method.

Right: Tulips in a vase.

Left: Tulips in a vase.

Below Left: Floral Plate.

Below Right: Plate using a resist method.

Daffodil Plate.

DAFFODIL PLATE

Method

1. Paint star and half star shapes to represent daffodils all over the plate in rich yellow and orange yellow.
2. Paint the stems and vase in Victoria green.
3. When dry, paint over the stems with leaf green, to give a two-tone effect.
4. Paint the lower third of the plate in turquoise and leave to dry for two hours.
5. Paint dots of cherry red all over the plate except on the vase and flowers.
6. Paint small mauve dashes on the vase.
7. When dry, paint orange yellow blobs in the centres of the rich yellow flowers and white blobs in the centres of the orange yellow flowers.

Materials

CERAMIC PAINTS:
rich yellow
orange yellow
Victoria green
leaf green
turquoise
cherry red
mauve
Brush no. 3
White plate

TRADITIONAL TEAPOT WITH BORDER

Method

1. Paint the simple flower shape freehand around the border of the teapot and lid. Don't worry if the leaves and dots are not identical — this adds to its individuality. Leave to dry.
2. If you have matching tea cups, why not extend the pattern around the rims of the cups and saucers?

Materials

White ceramic paint
Brush no. 3
Brown teapot

BLACK AND WHITE LAMP

The design inspiration for this shade and base comes from a carrier bag which a friend of mine was carrying. The stunning result owes more to the strong contrast of the black and white than it does to the free-flowing forms which make up the pattern.

Method

1. Draw the outline of the design onto the lamp base with a chinagraph pencil.
2. Fill in the zig zag shapes with ceramic paint in even strokes. A tip to ensure an even coat of paint is to fill the brush with lots of paint so you don't get brush strokes.
3. For the lampshade draw the design with light coloured tailor's chalk. Alternatively, you can make a pattern the shape of the shade out of tracing paper and draw the design on this. You can then place the tracing paper inside the shade and trace off the design onto the outside of the lampshade.
4. Paint the design with the black fabric paint and heat set it briefly with a hairdryer.
5. For even more impact, why not place the lamp on a similarly decorated surface? (see p. 39 below left).

Materials

Black ceramic paint
Black fabric paint
Brush no. 4
White lamp base and shade
Chinagraph pencil

Black and White Lamp.

BLUE LAMP WITH DOT PATTERN

Method

1. With a fine brush paint a repeated pattern of dots in white ceramic paint on the lamp base.
2. Repeat the pattern in reverse on the white shade, using the dark blue Setaskrib felt tip. Heat set briefly with a hairdryer.
3. Try drawing dots in other combinations to achieve different results.

Materials

White ceramic paint
Dark blue Setaskrib fabric marking pen
Brush no. 3
Small lamp base and shade

Opposite: Teapot.

Right: Dot pattern for Blue Lamp.

Below Left: Black and White Lamp.

Below Right: Blue Lamp.

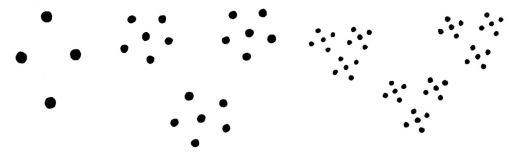

FLORAL LAMP BASE

This lamp has been painted with a floral design to co-ordinate with the curtains next to it.

Method

1. Undercoat the lamp base. Leave to dry.
2. Paint with eggshell white. Leave to dry.
3. Copy the design onto the base using a soft pencil.
4. Paint the design using brushes nos. 1 to 5, changing to the smallest numbers for the fine details.
5. Leave to dry for at least three or four days since artists' oils take a long time to dry.

Materials

Undercoat' (eggshell)
ARTIST'S OIL PAINTS:
Match to the fabric you have and mix colours where necessary.
You will be able to achieve a similiar, glossier result with ceramic paints
BRUSHES
1 — 5
Lamp base

CANDLESTICKS

Method

1. Mix black and white paint to form various shades of grey.
2. Paint feather motif in grey.
3. Mix grey with red to produce the dark red for the ribbons and flowers.

Materials

CERAMIC PAINTS:
black
white
ruby red
Brush no. 2
Plain ceramic candlesticks

Above: Candlesticks.

Below:
Top Left: Cactus Mug.

Top Right: Tulip Mug.

Bottom Left: Geometric Mug.

Bottom Right: Green Leaf Mug.

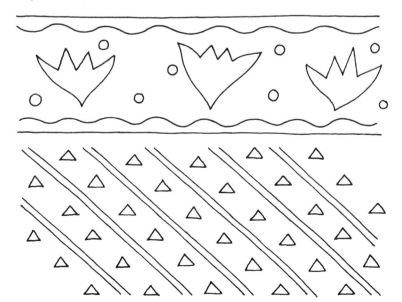

Left: Floral Lamp.

Below: Candlesticks.

WAVEY LINE MUG

Method

1. Paint short freehand waves alternately in blue, mauve and lavender. Wait until dry.
2. Stick reinforcement rings in a regular pattern over the mug and paint centres with alternating pink and black dots.

Materials

CERAMIC PAINTS:
Sevres blue
mauve
lavender
cyclamen pink
black
Brush no. 3
Reinforcement rings
Plain white mug

BRIGHT CACTUS MUG

Method

1. Make a stencil from the masking film and attach to the mug.
2. Apply the cactus shapes in mauve.
3. Paint the green wavy lines on top and bottom rims. Leave to dry.
4. Stick reinforcement rings onto the mug and paint orange dots in the centres using these as stencils.
5. When paint is dry remove film and reinforcements.

Materials

CERAMIC PAINTS:
Victoria green
mauve
orange
Low tack soft peel masking film
Brush no. 3
Reinforcement rings
Plain white mug

TULIP MUG

Method	Materials
1. Make a stencil from the film and attach to the mug. 2. Paint in tulip heads in pink. Leave to dry. 3. Paint stems and leaves in green. 4. Remove stencil when the paint is completely dry.	*CERAMIC PAINTS:* *cyclamen pink* *Victoria green* *Low tack soft peel masking film* *Brush no. 3* *Plain white mug*

GEOMETRIC MUG

Method	Materials
1. Cover the mug in strips of masking tape, leaving 5mm gaps between strips to make an even design. 2. Paint in the gaps with lavender. Leave to dry. 3. Remove the masking tape and stick on the triangle stencil. 4. Paint triangles in cherry red. 5. Remove stencil when the paint is dry.	*CERAMIC PAINTS:* *lavender* *cherry red* *Brush no. 3* *Masking tape* *Stationery stencil* *Plain white mug*

GREEN LEAF MUG

Method	Materials
1. Paint the central stem first, then add pear-shaped dabs of green for the leaves. 2. Rotate the mug, painting each leaf in turn.	*Victorian green ceramic paint* *Brush no. 3* *Plain white mug*

Black and White Crockery.

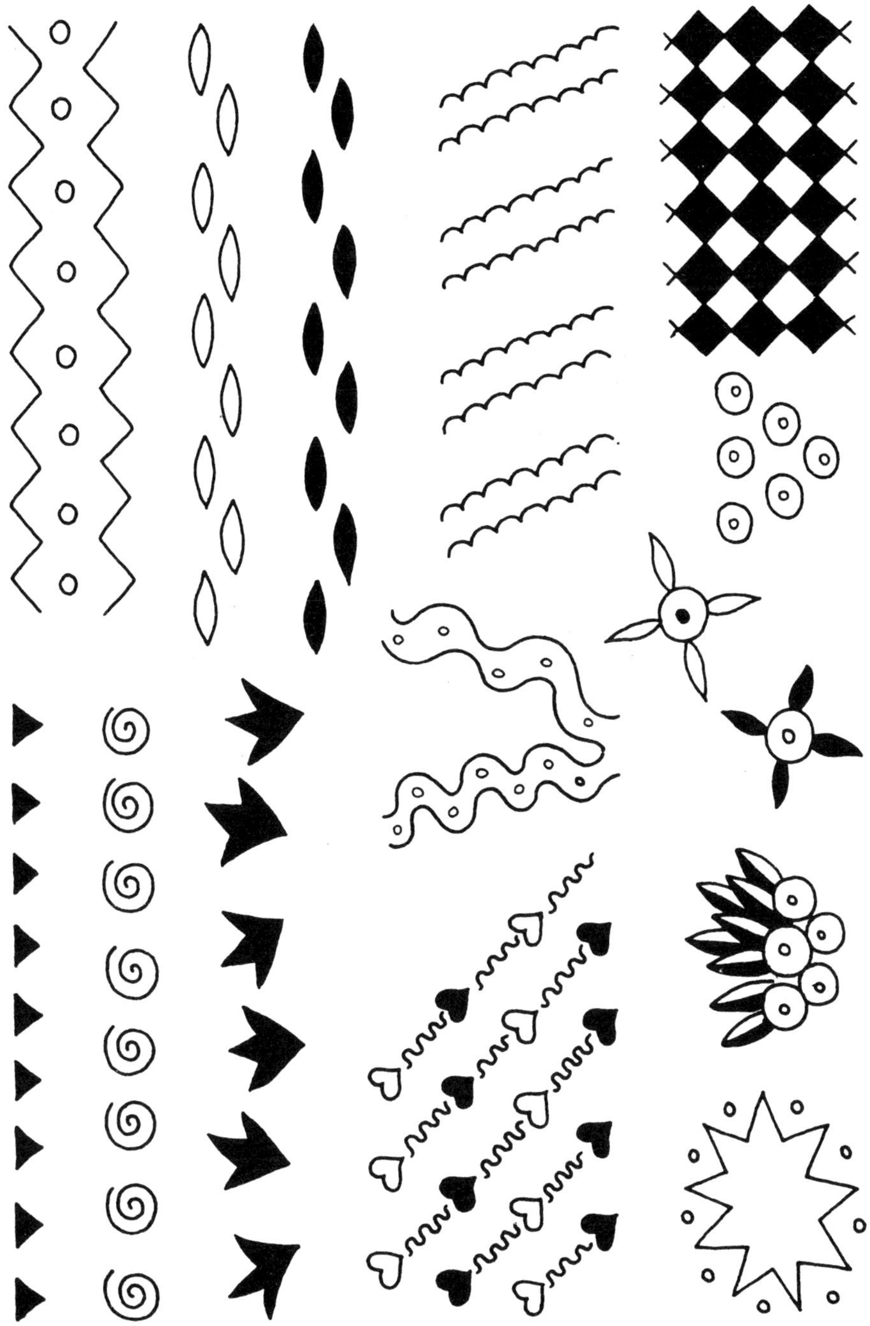

BLACK AND WHITE CROCKERY

Method

1. Paint or trace these geometric and floral patterns in combinations you like.
2. Why not develop your own freehand designs, or use bright red or blue instead of black?

Materials

Black ceramic paint
Brush no. 1.
Milk jug
Coffee cup and saucer
Tea cup and saucer
Egg cups

*Opposite: Black and White
Crockery.*

*Right: Pineapple Plate and Mugs
(for kitchenware see p. 101)*

PINEAPPLE PLATE AND MUGS

Method

1. Fix stencil to centre of plate.
2. Paint body of pineapple in lemon yellow.
3. Touch up middle sections with a coat of orange yellow.
4. Paint stem and very bottom green.
5. When paint is dry, remove stencil.
6. For the mugs, paint a smaller version of the design freehand in zig zags of lemon yellow.
7. Add a touch of green to the bottom of the fruit, and paint the stem green.

Materials

CERAMIC PAINTS:
lemon yellow
orange yellow
Victoria green
Brush no. 3
Stencil paper or low tack masking film
White plate and mugs

Pineapple Plate and Mugs.

FLOWER VASE TILES

Method

1. Paint this freehand, keeping the shapes simple and the colours bright and clean.
2. For similiar ideas look at seed packets for inspiration.

Materials

CERAMIC PAINTS:
orange
orange yellow
cyclamen pink
cherry red
lavender blue
emerald green
Victoria green
Sevres blue
Brush no. 2
4 plain ceramic tiles

Flower Vase.

Opposite: Flower Vase Tiles.

Right: Clown Tiles.

Below: Fish Tiles.

Clown Tiles.

CLOWN TILES

Method

1. Another very bright and bold design to paint freehand, using simple shapes.
2. Alternatively, trace the design from the template and outline the shape in pencil before starting to paint.

Materials

CERAMIC PAINTS: as for *Flower Vase Tiles (p. 49)*
Brush no. 3
4 plain ceramic tiles

Fish Tiles.

FISH TILES

Method

1. Attach stencil to first tile securely.
2. Mix blue and mauve together.
3. Dip brush into paint, then dab it onto spare paper until the brush is nearly dry.
4. Paint fish through stencil. The dryness of the paint makes a slightly mottled pattern, enhancing the fish scales in the design.
5. When paint is dry, remove stencil and turn upside down onto adjoining tile. Repeat steps 1-4.
6. For variety, change the proportion of blue and mauve as you repeat the design over four tiles.

Materials

CERAMIC PAINTS:
Sevres blue
mauve
Stencil paper
Stencil brush no. 2
Ceramic tiles

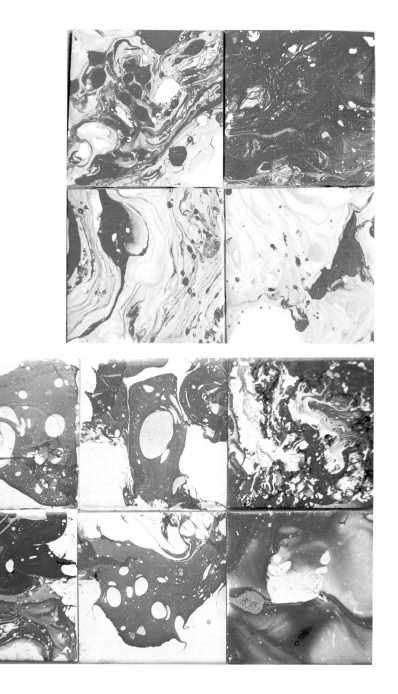

MARBLED TILES

Method

1. Pour a few drops of paint onto water. Blow gently to diffuse, then quickly dip tiles face down into bowl. Lift out immediately to dry. For further details of marbling see p. 116 and the pictures on p. 118.

Materials

CERAMIC PAINTS:
1:
emerald green
leaf green
2:
Sevres blue
gold
3:
orange
yellow
cherry red
Bowl of water
White spirit

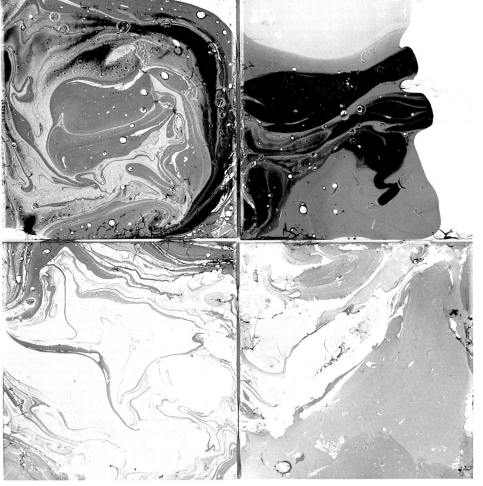

GLASS PAINTS

As well as decorating your crockery, why not turn your hand to glassware? Storage jars, glasses and decorative panels can all be enlivened by simple yet ingenious means. Ideas can be derived from art deco style, Victorian pub mirrors and stained glass windows and geometric designs can turn the dullest object into a masterpiece.

I've used the Pebeo transparent stained glass paints 'Couleurs Vitrails' in these glass projects, though other makes of glass paint could be used. Check the manufacturer's instructions before you begin, as always. To achieve an opaque effect in some of the projects, I've use ceramic paints, which also work well on glass. These are specified in each project, all other paints in this chapter are stained glass paints. If the colours are too strong you can tone down 'Couleurs Vitrails' by mixing them with 'Vernis Vitrails'.

SOME BEGINNERS' TIPS

1 **To outline a design**
   It is easiest to purchase a lead relief non-toxic outliner — I used Pebeo's 'Cerne Relief Vitrail' which can be applied directly from the tube nozzle. Take care that the outline is completely joined so that no paint can seep through. The outline takes 2-3 hours to dry.

2 **To colour in areas of a design**
   When the relief outline is dry, apply the glass paint with a clean, soft sable brush well loaded with paint. The paint will flow onto the glass without leaving brush strokes. 'Push' the paint gently to the edges if necessary. The paint can be thinned with white spirit if necessary.

3 **To make paler shades**
   Mix stained glass varnish with the paints, or mix the paints themselves together. You can also mix solvent-based glass and ceramic paints together to increase variety.

4 **Candles**
   Stained glass and ceramic paints can also be used to paint candles. Allow 48 hours for the paint to dry. Give the painted

candles a final protective coat by dipping them in clear melted wax.

5 It is vital to have both your brush and the glass surface clean. Clean brushes in white spirit and dry before starting work — water in the brush will produce bubbles in the paint.

6 Use the paints with stencils, sprays and for marbling.

PAINTED 'RUMPTOPF' JARS

Method (the same for both jars)

1. With the jar on its side and following the raised design already stamped on it as a guide, dip the brush into the paint and let the colour flow onto the shapes in the glass. You should not overload your brush — you will find that the paint will automatically stop at the raised edges. On the other hand don't keep the brush too dry as this will mean making unnecessary brush strokes.
2. Try not to 'work' the paint too much.
3. Leave the first side to dry for at least 24 hours before turning the jar over to paint the next side.

Materials

GLASS PAINTS:
Left hand jar:
crimson (for cherries and their border pattern and raspberries)
yellow (for the pears, their border and the flowers)
red/violet (for the plums and their stems and their border)
chartreuse green for all the leaves and remaining stems
Right hand jar:
red/violet (for the plums)
emerald green (for the plum leaves)
brown (for all the stems)
black (for all the border designs)
crimson red (for the cherries)
chartreuse green (for the cherry and pear leaves)
orange (for the pears)
Brush no. 3
2 Rumptopf jars

Above: Rumptopf Jars.

Below: Jam Jars.

Opposite: Cocktail Glasses, Tumbler and Water Jug.

JAM JARS

Method

1. To paint the dots on the left and central jars, stick on reinforcement rings as stencils. Paint in red-violet or orange as required.
2. To achieve the triangular and oblong patterns (second from left and right), stick masking tape onto the jars leaving the required shape blank. Painting with a ceramic paint, as here, gives an opaque rather than a transparent finish.
3. For the zig zag shapes on the three pasta filled jars, paint a solid line of black paint as an outline and leave to dry. Then apply the orange, red-violet and yellow paint liberally — the rim of paint will contain the area coloured.

Materials

GLASS PAINTS:
red-violet
black
orange
crimson
yellow
Sevres blue ceramic paint
Brush no. 4
Reinforcement rings
Outliner
Masking tape

COCKTAIL GLASSES, TUMBLER AND WATER JUG

Method

1. Stick the reinforcement rings on all the items in a pattern of your choice.
2. For the jug, tumbler and black stemmed cocktail glass, paint black spots through the stencils. Leave to dry.
3. For the red stemmed cocktail glass, paint red spots through the stencils. I also painted the stem of this glass with a coat of red paint.
4. Once dry, remove stencils.

Materials

GLASS PAINTS:
black
crimson
Brush no. 3
2 cocktail glasses
Reinforcement rings
Tumbler
Water jug

CUP AND SAUCER PLUS GLASS AND TRAYCLOTH

Method

1. Place fabric on a flat surface and secure each side with tape or pins. The fabric should be as taut as possible.
2. Slip a piece of blotting paper under the area you wish to stencil. Place stencil in place and secure with tape. (Alternatively, lightly pencil your design onto the fabric.)
3. Colour in the design using the fabric pens.
4. When the design is dry, heat set the paint on both sides with the iron set for cotton for about half a minute each side. Use a cooler iron for a longer time with polyester mixtures.

For the Glass

1. Draw design on a small piece of paper and place inside the glass. The design will show through and you can use the outlines for painting using the ceramic paint.
2. Alternatively paint freehand or use a chinagraph pencil for the central stem of the leaf and the design outline.
3. When the ceramic paint is completely dry (at least 24 hours) remove chinagraph pencil with white spirit.
4. Decorate cup and saucer using the chinagraph method as above.

Materials

Traycloth material — preferably cotton
SETASKRIB FABRIC MARKERS light green and yellow
Stencil
Low tack adhesive film
CERAMIC PAINTS
leaf green
cherry red
pale yellow
white spirit
Brush no. 3
Cup and Saucer
Wine glass

Stained Glass Panels.
(Based on a design featured in
Matsuya Piece-Goods Store:
JAPANESE DESIGN MOTIFS,
Dover Publications, Inc., New York,
1972.)

STAINED GLASS PANELS

Method

1. Trace the design onto paper the same size as the panel.
2. Clean the glass surface with warm water and washing up liquid to remove any surface grease. Rinse and dry thoroughly or clean with white spirit.
3. Lie the glass panel on top of the design.
4. Trace the lines of the design using lead relief outliner. Hold the tube at a slight angle to the glass and squeeze it evenly and gently. The action should be as if you are 'laying' the outliner onto the glass.
5. Keep a tissue near at hand to wipe away any excess outliner from the nozzle of the tube. This avoids initial blobs.
6. Leave the outliner to dry for two to four hours before applying the paint. This process may be speeded up by placing the glass on a warm radiator, protected by paper.
7. Put a piece of white paper behind the panel so you can see when applying colour that it is spreading evenly.
8. Mix equal quantities of the varnish and glass paint. Apply to glass with a brush letting the paint flow freely from the brush. Start in the centre and 'push' paint to the edges. Do not overwork the paint. Applied like this the paint appears dry after 24 hours but actually takes several days to dry completely.

Materials

GLASS PAINTS:
crimson
emerald green
deep blue
turquoise
orange
Brush no. 5
Lead relief outliner
Varnish for toning down the
colours
2 circles of glass

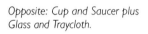

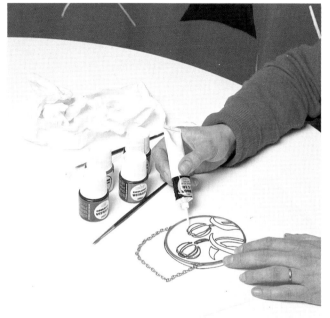

Opposite: Cup and Saucer plus Glass and Traycloth.

Above left and right: Stained Glass Panels.

Centre: Painting Glass.

METAL AND WOOD PAINTS

Ceramic, glass and acrylic paints are all suitable for wood and have different finishes depending on what you are decorating.

The ceramic paints give an enamelled finish when used on metal, for example the kitchen scales and the canal boat tin.

For a semi-opaque effect mix the glass and the ceramic paints together.

Pebeo make a fluid, fast-drying, non-toxic acrylic paint called Light Deco which is ideal for painting wooden surfaces. This can be used on natural or painted wood. If you wish to preserve the wood grain and natural colour, prime the wood with Vernis à la Cire diluted with white spirit, or a similar wax varnish.

To give a transparent effect dilute the Light Deco with water.

BLACK LACQUER BOX

Method

1. With a compass lightly draw two concentric circles in the centre of the box. The centre can be found by halving the length and width of the box. Then make marks at 12 o'clock, 4 and 8 o'clock. The design is drawn from these points.
2. Pencil in other designs on three sides and where the design is halved (on opening the box) continue these lines inside, down and along the base of the box. These lines when painted give an attractive stripey effect inside the box.
3. Pour some black acrylic paint into a saucer and mix with a little water. You want an even consistency of paint which flows onto the box. With your brush, paint the background of the box doing the top first and then the sides. The paint dries very quickly and you will not have to wait long before turning the box on its side. Once you have done this, open the box and paint the inside black leaving the pattern continuation stripes blank for the moment. Wash your brush immediately in water. *This is most important* as acrylic paints are impervious to water when dry. Dry your brush with a rag and apply the next colour. Some details may have to be accentuated with black using a *very* fine squirrel hairbrush.

Materials

ACRYLIC PAINTS:
black
yellow ochre
golden yellow
turtledove grey
moss green
gold
Garance madder
Patina varnish
Old saucers for mixing paints
Water for diluting paint
if needed
Fine sandpaper
Pencil and compass for design
Brushes nos. 6 and 3 and
00/2 fine squirrel hair
Whitewood (or any other) box

*Black Lacquer Box.
(Based on a design featured in Ed Sibbett, Jr.: ORNAMENTAL FLOWER STAINED GLASS PATTERN BOOK, Dover Publications, Inc., New York, 1984.)*

4. When it comes to painting the inside stripes, just continue the same colour over the rim and down the inside edges of the box following your original pencilled stripes.

5. To give a lacquered look, with a good quality wide flat brush (this is quicker and gives more even coverage than a round pointed brush) and using Vernis à Patiner, evenly cover as much of the box as you can. A thin even layer is much more successful than a thick layer which may leave 'run' marks. After 24 hours you can apply varnish to the remaining areas but be careful not to leave finger marks! If your brush or room was dusty you may have to sand down the box — don't be alarmed when you lose the lovely glossy look. It will return when you apply your second coat of varnish.

6. Continue to apply as many coats as you feel necessary, sanding in between if you wish. I applied three coats.

7. Clean your varnish brush with white spirit and try to wait at least four days before varnishing inside. When you have varnished inside (I used a matt satin varnish called Vernis à la Cire) leave the box open for a few days to dry completely. The box is now resistant to scratches, alcohol, etc.

Left: Black Lacquer Box.

Opposite: Crackle Box.

CRACKLE BOX

Method

1. The box seemed to lend itself to the style of early American Folk Art, which was the inspiration for these designs. The box was in pre-cut sections and was painted before assembling.
2. Lightly pencil the design on each section using the compass if you find it helpful. Paint your design, diluting the paint with a very little water. Over painting (for example the little black dots in centre of large flower) can be done immediately the first layer is dry.
3. After a couple of minutes you can varnish the box in sections, as I did, or you can assemble the box before varnishing. Either way, with a wide, flexible, natural hair brush place a smooth coat of patina varnish over the whole area. After at least 12 hours brush on another even layer of patina varnish. Wait until this is *just* 'dry to the touch'. This very much depends on room temperature and thickness of varnish —generally between 4-12 hours but you can speed things up by placing the object in an airing cupboard (be careful of fluff) or by placing it on or near a warm radiator. If the radiator is too hot the wood may warp.

Materials

ACRYLIC PAINTS:
moss green
Garance madder
purple
black
yellow ochre
Patina varnish
Crackle varnish
White spirit for cleaning brushes
Pencil
Sanding paper (fine)
Brush no. 3
Whitewood box
Saucer for mixing
A compass is useful

3. When the second layer of varnish is 'dry to the touch' apply with a different brush, an even layer of Vernis à Craqueler. Again, depending on room temperature, the crackles will automatically appear after 15 to 20 minutes. If the varnish does not crackle your room is too cold! Try again but thoroughly wash off the old crackling varnish with water before applying a new layer. It is always wise to do a test piece first. Clean your brush with water. The crackles appear because the Vernis à Craqueler is water based and Vernis à Patiner is solvent based. The two varnishes dry at different rates.

4. Once the varnish is dry, you will want to colour the crackles to make the object appear old. This can be done with Couleurs Vitrails glass paint. Add a tiny amount of brown solvent based glass paint to some white spirit. With a soft brush 'wash' this mixture over and into the crackles removing the excess spirit mixture with a tissue or cloth until you have the amount of staining you require. When dry, brush one or two final layers of Vernis à Patiner over the whole object which will then be water and stain resistant.

*Opposite: Crackle Box.
(Based on a design featured in
Joseph D'Addetta: AMERICAN
FOLK ART DESIGNS AND
MOTIFS FOR ARTISTS AND
CRAFTSPEOPLE, Dover
Publications, Inc., New York,
1984.)*

*Left: Wooden Box with Floral
Design.*

WOODEN BOX WITH FLORAL DESIGN

Method

1. Trace the design onto box, or lightly draw freehand in pencil.
2. Paint in mauve flowers and green stalks, diluting part with a little water.
3. When dry, draw on black markings with Setaskrib pen or use black paint with a fine brush.

Materials

*CERAMIC OR ACRYLIC
PAINTS:
Light Deco
light green
mauve
Setaskrib black fabric pen
Brush no. 2
Small box*

Left: Wooden Box with Floral Design.

Below: Scales.

SCALES

Method

1. Paint the base of the scales with an even coat of black. Leave to dry.
2. Paint the dish with silver.
3. When the base is dry stick stencils of brightly coloured folk art design to one side of base. Paint in motifs as in the photograph opposite.
4. When the paint is dry, remove stencil and repeat on the other side of the base.

Materials

CERAMIC PAINTS:
black
silver
cherry red
lavender blue
Victoria green
orange yellow
Brush no. 3
Old fashioned pair of scales

Letter Rack.

LETTER RACK

Method

1. Stick stencil onto front of letter rack. Paint motifs as in the photograph (p. 74).
2. When dry, remove stencil, and repeat design on the back part of the rack.
3. Paint freehand around the holes for screws.

Materials

CERAMIC OR ACRYLIC PAINTS:
lavender blue
cherry red
Victoria green
mauve
Stencils
Brush no. 3
Letter rack

DECORATING FURNITURE

Method

Decorating furniture is fun and very rewarding. Acrylic paint will dry in about three minutes on unprimed wood. It takes a little longer (half an hour to an hour) on non-absorbent surfaces. It very much depends how thickly you apply it and how much water you add to it. When dry, all acrylics are difficult to remove, because they become waterproof. Light Deco is a fluid, extremely dense paint and Artists' Acrylic paint is of a much thicker consistency and, unless very much diluted with water, will give a raised effect similar to artists' oil colours. Adversely, when diluted with water they will lose their 'covering power'.

Before you start you need the right sort of surface to paint onto.

UNPAINTED WOOD

You may wish to keep the item of furniture you are painting plain wood and give it a decorative painted finish of, for example, flowers (photo p. 75).

Before painting on furniture you should:
1. Fill any holes with wood filler.
2. Rub the surface down with sandpaper.
3. Clean the surface of the wood with a cloth dampened in white spirit, to remove any grease or dirt.
4. Draw the design onto the surface with a soft pencil.
5. Paint your design using acrylic or artists' oil paints.
6. Leave to dry for at least three days before varnishing if you are using oil paints. Acrylic paints will dry in minutes.

PAINTING ONTO A BACKGROUND COLOUR

If the furniture is already painted but has a bumpy uneven texture or you wish to change the background colour you should:
1. Rub the uneven surface with sandpaper until smooth.
2. Fill any holes with wood filler.
3. Paint any bare patches of wood with primer (e.g. Vernis à la Cire mixed half in half with white spirit). This stops any subsequent coats of paint from sinking into the wood.
4. Paint on a coat of undercoat. This gives a matt even colour.

Letter Rack.

5. Sand using a 500 grain sandpaper.
6. Paint with eggshell paint, as this is an ideal surface to decorate.
7. When the eggshell is dry, sand and then paint on another coat.
8. Decorate with acrylic or artists' oils.
9. Leave at least three days before varnishing.

STRIPPED PINE CHEST OF DRAWERS

Garlands of tiny flowers were painted round the handles of this plain stripped pine chest of drawers. Slightly larger flowers were painted onto the corner of each drawer. The final result is very pretty.

Method

1. Paint the flowers directly onto chest of drawers in a wreath effect around the handles.
2. As an alternative, you could create a pretty design on pine using stencils.

Materials

OIL OR ACRYLIC PAINTS:
lilac
purples
grey/blue
pale pink
fuscia pink
assorted greens for leaves

Above: Stripped Pine Chest of Drawers.

Below: Floral Chest of Drawers.

FLORAL CHEST OF DRAWERS

Method	Materials
1. Paint a base coat of cream evenly over the chest of drawers. Leave to dry.	OIL OR ACRYLIC PAINTS:
	cream
2. Mix yellow ochre and brown paints, and thin with an oil-based glaze. Apply to the chest, giving a stippled effect. Leave to dry.	yellow ochre
	brown
	shades of pastel pink, blue, lilac,
3. Either trace floral pattern, or paint it freehand, using colours as in photograph (p. 75 below).	green yellow
	Oil based glaze
	Chest of drawers

GEOMETRIC TRESTLE TABLE

Method	Materials
1. Sand down the door to make an even finish.	ACRYLIC PAINTS:
2. Stick masking tape down on the surface to create geometric squares and triangles of space.	blue
	orange
	white
3. Fill in the shapes, by sponging in the acrylic paint, diluted with water.	Masking tape
	Sponge
4. When dry, remove masking tape.	Brush no. 6
5. Finish with a coat of varnish to give durability.	Varnish
	For the table:
	One flush door
	Metal trestle stands

ROCKING CHAIR

Method	Materials
1. Paint chair with white paint. Leave to dry.	ACRYLIC PAINTS:
2. Draw ribbon and rose design onto chair in pencil.	white
	purple
3. Mix purple and white paints to produce a variety of pink and purple shades, and paint in design.	Small rocking chair
	Brush no. 3

Stripped Pine Chest of Drawers.

Right: Trestle Table.

Opposite: Rocking Chair.

PAINTING ON ENAMELWARE

Much of the inspiration for this kind of work comes from old gypsy caravans and canal boat art. Enamel-painted tin is still popular in China, with the use of amazing colours with lush and sentimental paintings of roses, strange Chinese birds, cockerels and pandas. Design ideas are also to be found in work of the Slavonic nations of Eastern Europe.

BEGINNERS' TIPS

1. It is a good idea to practise painting on an old tin or oil can before embarking on your first project.
2. Try painting on enamelware from hardware stores — mugs, coffee pots, teapots, saucepans, etc. Pieces with a brightly coloured background are most suitable for the canal style of painting; those with a white background are better for the Chinese.
3. Do not mix different types of paints for enamelware, as these are sometimes incompatible and one may dissolve another. You may of course mix different colours.
4. I used the Pebeo Ceramic à Froid for the following projects. Alternatively you could use cellulose paints (those used for painting cars in a liquid paint or spray form); enamel paints (use a large pot for the background colour and smaller pots of model-makers' colours for the foreground); or gloss paints (both undercoat and primer).

OTHER MATERIALS

A selection of brushes
White spirit for washing brushes
Varnish
Sandpaper

1

paint tin black

DECORATED ENAMEL TIN

Method

I. Sand down the tin until it is smooth and clean.
2. Paint on the black background colour with the no. 6 brush in an even coat. When dry, sand with a fine grade sandpaper.
3. Paint on another coat with the no. 6 brush and leave to dry.
4. Paint background forms of the design freehand for the leaves and roses using brush no. 3. Leave to dry.
5. Paint petals and leaf markings with single swift brush strokes using brush no. 2. Leave to dry.
6. Add dots and dashes for the flower centres using brush no. 2. Leave to dry.
7. Finish with a coat of clear varnish.

Materials

CERAMIC PAINTS:
black
white
orange yellow
cherry red
lavender blue
leaf green
chamois
cyclamen pink
garnet red
Brushes nos. 2, 3 and 6
Enamel sweet tin
sandpaper

2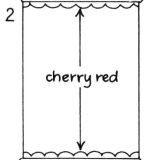

cherry red

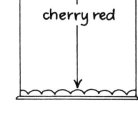 leaf green mixed with orange yellow

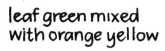 lavender

chamois

 cyclamen pink

FRONT

3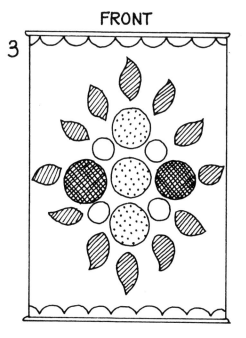

SIDE

4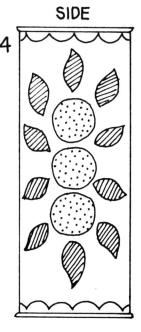

5 — garnet red

add rose petals – garnet down centre with at side

add daisy petals – white

— white

6

add yellow markings to leaves, centres of daisies and centre of roses

7

finish with white dots

pattern

flower dots
yellow centres

Right: Enamel Mug.

Below: Decorated Enamel Tin and Floral Bowl.

FLORAL BOWL

Method

1. Prepare bowl by sanding down as in enamel tin (p. 81).
2. Apply a coat of orange paint as background. Leave to dry and repeat.
3. Paint floral design as in enamel tin.

Materials

CERAMIC PAINTS:
orange
mauve
white
Sevres blue
rich yellow
black
Brush no. 6
Enamel bowl
Sandpaper

Floral Bowl.

ENAMEL MUG

The design for this mug owes more to mid-European folk art than it does to canal and gypsy art.

Method

1. Prepare the mug by sanding down and then coat with red paint. When dry, sandpaper and add another coat.
2. Outline floral shape in turquoise. Leave to dry.
3. Paint blue adjoining floral shapes. Leave to dry.
4. Add pattern of white dots around the design.

Materials

CERAMIC PAINTS:
cherry red
white
turquoise
lavender blue
Sandpaper
Brush no. 3
White spirit
Enamel mug (white)

 lavender 11

turquoise 16

Enamel Mug.

FABRIC PAINTS

There are many varieties of fabric paint available to the general public. When you are selecting, consider whether you want to paint or print onto a dark or light material. Some fabric paints sit on the cloth and do not absorb the background colour of the fabric, giving a true, strong colour. Other paints sink into the fabric, which is acceptable if the background is pale, but makes the colours look muddy if the fabric is dark.

I have used the Pebeo range of transparent and opaque paints in this chapter, which include fluorescent and pearl shades. Their fabric blender 'Coupure Incolore' can lighten the shade of a colour without changing the consistency of the paint. If you add water the consistency changes. If you add white you change the colour. For silk screen printing Pebeo produce the thickener 'Epaissant'. Other fabric paints are also suitable for the projects in this chapter — match the shades, or vary them if you wish, and follow the manufacturer's instructions carefully.

Pebeo also produce a range of non-toxic Setaskrib fabric marking pens. These are designed for painting and drawing on cottons, synthetics, some lycra and silk. When heat set by ironing the colours can be washed or dry cleaned. The felt tip is a tapered point which allows you to paint both thin and thick lines and also to shade areas. Refill bottles with a dropper (which should be applied through the felt tip) are available together with replaceable felt tips. These pens are very easy to use, will not stiffen the fabric and are suitable for decorating lampshades, blinds, table linen and tee shirts, etc.

WAVY LINE DECK CHAIR COVERS

Method

1. For the left-hand chair, paint a curvy line of blue the length of the fabric. Leave to dry.
2. Paint a parallel line of pink in the centre of the fabric.
3. When dry, paint the third line in green.
4. Iron the fabric to set the colours.
5. Clean and sand down the wooden frames. Paint white or blue.
6. Attach the new cover with upholsterer's tacks.
7. Repeat for the right-hand chair using fluorescent green, yellow and vermillion.

Materials

TRANSPARENT FABRIC PAINTS:
ultra marine blue
fluorescent pink
light green
fluorescent green
buttercup yellow
vermillion

ACRYLIC PAINTS
white
blue
length of canvas
upholsterer's tacks
1in./2.5cm decorator's brush
deckchair frames

Wavy Line Deck Chair Covers.

PATCHY DECK CHAIR COVERS

Method

1. Prepare wooden frames as above.
2. Rip holes in the newspaper and use it as a stencil. Attach to canvas and sponge colours through the holes.
3. For the left-hand canvas mask off top and bottom sections with newspaper. Paint a band of yellow over the green paper shapes.
4. Heat set canvas with an iron.
5. Attach canvas to deck chair as above.

Materials

FABRIC PAINTS:
green
yellow
white
Sponge (natural)
Newspaper
Length of white canvas
Length of blue canvas
Deck chair frames
Upholstery tacks
Gloves

BLUE WAVY DESIGN

Method

1. Draw broken wavy lines freehand diagonally on canvas.
2. Alternatively draw the design on in tailor's chalk or soft pencil and then paint over with Setaskrib. Heat set.
3. Attach canvas to deck chair as above.

Materials

FABRIC PAINTS:
blue Setaskrib fabric pen
Length of white canvas
Upholstery tacks
Blue painted deck chair frame

POT PLANT BLIND

This design was taken from some Victorian tiles surrounding a fire place.

Method

1. Trace or copy the design onto the blind using a soft pencil.
2. When satisfied, go over design with Setaskrib pen and heat set with an iron.

Materials

Setaskrib fabric pens in brown, grey, yellow, orange
Plain blind

Pot Plant Blind.

Above: Patchy Deck Chair Covers.

Below: Blue Wavy Design.

Pot Plant Blind.

Red Abstract Blind.

RED ABSTRACT BLIND

Method

1. Draw outline of the design with tailor's chalk.
2. Colour in the shapes and squiggles, applying one colour at a time. Wait for each colour to dry before applying the next.
3. When paint is dry, heat set with an iron.

Materials

OPAQUE FABRIC PAINTS:
black
buttercup yellow
cobalt blue
light green
lemon yellow
white
Brush no. 6
Tailor's chalk
Red blind

PALE BLUE PEARL BLIND

Method

1. Lay masking tape onto the blind to form triangular stencils.
2. Press down the edges of the tape firmly with the back of a spoon to prevent the paint from leaking under the edges.
3. Paint triangles by sponging on one colour at a time. Wait for each colour to dry before applying the next.
4. When all paint is dry, remove masking tape, and heat set with an iron.

Materials

PEARLIZED OR NACRE FABRIC PAINTS:
lapis lazuli
aquamarine
jade
pearl
Masking tape
Sponge (natural)
Pale blue blind

DUVET COVER AND PILLOWCASE

A design based on the paintings of Mondrian.

Method

1. Wash fabric to remove manufacturer's dressing. Iron and lie taut over a board to absorb excess paint.
2. Stick masking tape onto fabric to form stencils of rectangles and lines.

Materials

OPAQUE FABRIC PAINTS:
black
white
Sponge (natural)

Below: Duvet Cover.

Opposite left: Red Abstract Blind.

Right: Pale Blue Blind.

3. Fill in shapes with white and black paints using sponge.
4. For the white areas two coats might be needed to prevent the red fabric showing through.
5. When paint is dry, heat set with an iron.

Gloves
Masking tape
Plain red duvet cover and pillowcase

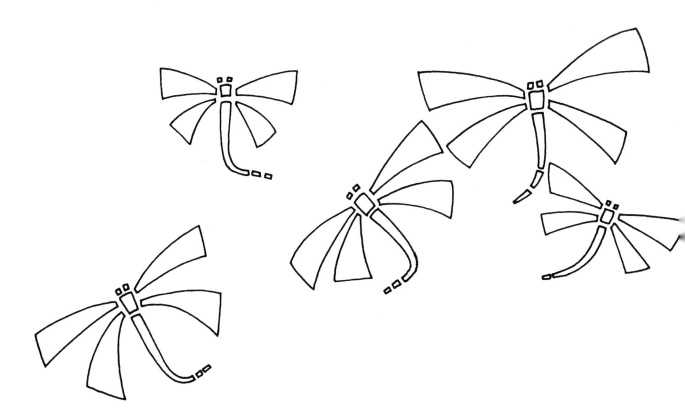

Dragonfly Curtains.

DRAGONFLY CURTAINS

Method

1. Wash and iron fabric to remove manufacturer's dressing. Lay flat on board or paper.
2. Attach stencil to the fabric with the larger dragonflies at the bottom and the smaller ones at the top.
3. Paint in dragonflies in alternate colours blue and green.
4. When the complete pattern is applied and dry, remove the stencil and clean and dry it thoroughly.
5. Flip the stencil so that the top two dragonflies can be printed in reverse.
6. Heat set paint by ironing.
7. Make up material into curtains.

Materials

PEARLIZED OR NACRE FABRIC PAINTS:
pearlized blue
pearlized green
Stencil
Grey fabric
Stencil Brush no. 6

WHITE TULIP LAMPSHADE AND BASE

This extremely simple design could be done in any colour to fit in with a bedroom scheme. Always put your plan on paper and use children's crayons to see if you like the colours.

Method

1. Make a paper pattern to 'fit' the shade. Slip it over the shade and see if you like the effect. Alternatively, lightly pencil your design onto the shade (having first practised on paper).
2. Colour the petals and light green leaves first and use the dark green to outline the leaves.
3. When dry, quickly heat set the shade with a hairdryer.
4. For the lamp base the same design was copied in miniature using ceramic paint. If you make a mistake just wipe your design away with a rag (you might need white spirit) and start again! Clean your brush and dry it between each colour.
5. The lamp base should be left to dry for at least 24 hours. (Photograph on p. 7.)

Materials

Plain white lamp base (though you could use other colours)
White lampshade (white is best as the Setaskrib pens will not show their true colours on other shades — if you are doing a design with black or navy this may not matter)
SETASKRIB FABRIC MARKING PENS: red, pink, light green, dark green, brown (for the shade)
CERAMIC PAINTS: cherry red, brown, Victoria green (for the base)
White spirit
Brush no. 3

RED GEOMETRIC CURTAINS

Method

1. Wash and iron fabric to remove manufacturer's dressing. Pin out on a board.
2. Stick masking tape onto fabric to make stencils for triangles and lines.
3. Sponge black setacolor into triangles. Leave to dry.
4. Sponge in white setacolor for the lines, allow to dry and heat set, with an iron.
5. Make fabric up into curtains.

Materials

OPAQUE FABRIC PAINTS:
black setacolor
white setacolor
Sponge (natural)
Gloves
Red fabric for curtains
Masking tape

Above: Dragonfly Curtains.

Opposite: Red Geometric Curtains.

BRIGHT BLUE CURTAINS

Method

1. Wash and iron fabric to remove manufacturer's dressing and stretch over board.
2. Lay masking tape onto the fabric to form a pattern of stripes.
3. Paint bold wavy lines freehand between lines of tape.
4. Cut potato to make a cross shape and a circle (see techniques, p. 117). Print motifs between the stripes of tape.
5. Make up into curtains.

Materials

OPAQUE FABRIC PAINTS:
parma violet
light green
vermillion
buttercup
cobalt blue
orange
Masking tape
Potato
½in/1.25cm decorator's brush
Potatoes
Blue fabric for curtains

Right: Bright Blue Curtains.

Below: Stencilled Cushions.

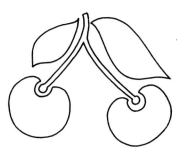

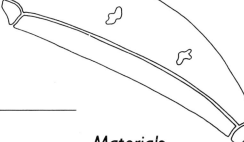

STENCILLED CUSHIONS

Method

1. Scale up the fruit templates to the size required. The pineapple template is on p. 48.
2. Cut three stencils (see p. 112) for the strawberries and two each for the banana and cherries for the different areas of colour.
3. Paint the background colour first and dry with a hair dryer before adding the details.

Materials

FABRIC PAINTS
lemon yellow
orange yellow
brown
light green
vermillion
stencil
stencil brush
blue polycotton material

Kitchenware and Table Linen.

KITCHENWARE AND TABLE LINEN

Method

1. Fix stencil to the fabric firmly.
2. Paint in coffee cup design.
3. When dry, remove stencil, and heat set with an iron.
(The photograph for this appears on p. 47.)

Materials

Setacolor blue opaque fabric paint
Stencil
Brush no. 4
Stencil
Tea towels
Apron
Oven mittens

PINEAPPLE TABLECLOTH AND NAPKINS

Method

1. Make a large pineapple stencil (see p. 48) for the tablecloth and smaller ones for the napkins.
2. Fold the tablecloth in half and then half again, and then half again. Place pins to mark the eight fold lines.
3. Lay out the pineapple stencil so that the stalks face towards the centre, with four in the middle and eight round the edge (depending on size). Fill in the stencil with paint brush.
4. Fill out the central design by adding green leaves once the stencils are removed.
5. Print small pineapples in the corners of the napkins.

Materials

OPAQUE FABRIC PAINTS:
lemon yellow
buttercup yellow
light green
Stencil brush no. 6
Stencils
Royal blue tablecloth and napkins

Left: Bright Blue Curtains.

Below: Stencilled Cusions.

Opposite: Pineapple Table Cloth and Napkins.

SILK PAINTING

Traditional and professional silk paints are easy to use but the steaming method of fixing them can seem daunting to the beginner. For these silk projects I used Pebeo Orient Express silk dyes, except in one case where I used Setacolor Transparent fabric paint. Orient Express does not have to be steam fixed. The range of colours can be mixed together and diluted with water, and used on either wool or silk. Unlike similar silk paints, these are concentrated fade-resistant dyes which produce vibrant colours, and are non-toxic.

The gutta outline follows the same principle as the glass outliner, and comes in clear, black, gold or silver shades. It is a gum-like solution and when dry it acts as a barrier to the dyes, preventing the colours from diffusing into one another.

The applicator for the gutta is a plastic bottle with a nozzle at the end. Fill applicator with gutta using a paper funnel. Pierce the ball at the end of the nozzle from the inside with a pin to allow the gutta to flow through the hole. Alternatively a nib can be used which some people find easier.

Tips

1. To avoid air locks and bubbles, up-end the applicator vertically at regular intervals.
2. Clean the bottle and nozzle thoroughly after use with white spirit to prevent the nozzle becoming blocked up.
3. Add a few drops of gutta solvent if the gutta is too thick. The gutta should penetrate the silk right through to the back. If you add too much solvent, the gutta may bleed and will not act as a barrier to the dyes.
4. For a different coloured gutta, add a few drops of solvent based stained glass paint to the clear solvent based gutta.
5. Make sure that the fabric used is 100% silk or wool.
6. These paints may also be used for tie dye or batik. They may be mixed together, diluted with water or used with a diffuser.
7. If covering a large area of silk in one colour, add a few drops of diffusing agent to the Orient Express dye. This helps to avoid hard lines and gives even coverage.

Silk Paintings.

Below: Painting on Silk.

SILK PAINTINGS AND CUSHIONS

Opposite: Silk Paintings.

The designs for the cushions and paintings in the photos are shown on pp. 105 and 108, and the materials used for each project are listed below.

Left: Silk Cushion.

Below: Silk Painting.

Overleaf: Silk Cushions.

Method

1. Gently wash and dry silk to remove manufacturer's dressing. Experiment on a spare piece of prepared silk before starting.
2. Pin the silk or wool onto a batik frame stretching it as you pin. The best way to do this is to work from the centre of one side out to the edge, from the centre to the other edge. Turn the frame round and do the opposite side in the same way. Repeat for the other two sides.
3. Make your drawing the size of the finished article, making sure that it fits within the frame, in a heavy pencil or pen so that you can see it through the silk. Slip the drawing under the stretched silk and attach with Sellotape.
4. Fill the applicator with gutta. Do not cut off rounded end.
5. Trace your design onto silk with the applicator making sure that the tracing lines are completely joined with no gaps. It is important that the gutta penetrates the silk through to the back.
6. When the gutta is dry (about one hour), start to paint. Dip a good quality, soft brush into the silk paint and apply to the centre of each section to be painted. Add a little more dye if necessary but remember that silk will only accept a certain amount of dye. It will depend on the type and thickness of the silk used how the colour diffuses through the cloth, so experiment on a spare piece of silk before starting your painting.

Materials

Silk — varying weight and type will dictate the finished result
Frame
Pins
Paper
Waterproof marker
Liquid fixative
Gutta
Gutta applicator
Orient Express silk dye
Sellotape

BASIC TECHNIQUES

STENCILLING

Paper patterns, pierced with holes and stained with red earth paint, provide evidence of the earliest stencils. Dating back to the tenth century AD these were used to repeat the outline, over and over again, of the figures which line the caves of a Thousand Buddhas in Western China. However, stencilling was not extensively employed in Europe until the fifteenth century. It provided an accurate method of overlaying colour onto an otherwise black and white design. Playing cards and later wallpapers were originally coloured in this manner.

In the eighteenth century, American colonists used stencils as a cheaper alternative to the imported hand blocked wallpaper that only the very rich could afford. For their design inspiration they turned to natural forms such as willows, oak leaves, fruit and eagles.

Tips

Before working on large areas of cloth it is wise to practise on small pieces of closely woven fabric, or even paper, to get the feel for this craft.

The secret of successful stencilling is to apply the colour in small amounts, not allowing the paint to become too liquid, so that it doesn't seep under the edges of the stencil.

When stencilling it is important to make sure that the surface is properly cleaned so that the paint will adhere. In the case of fabric wash out the manufacturer's dressing. Remove wax from floors and furniture and scrub walls clean.

Design Sources

Look at ideas with lots of 'bridges' — 'bridges' are elements of design which help to hold the composition together by providing a framework for the motifs. Therefore basketwork, trellis, fish scales and skeletons are all ideal for stencil design. Good motifs are fruit, flowers and birds, but also icecream cornets and cones, and fairground architecture.

Making Stencils.

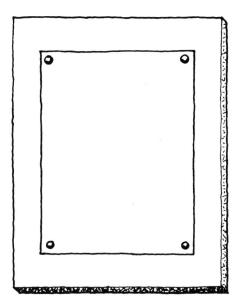

Making Stencils

Stencils can be bought ready-made, in book form or you can make them yourself. Good art suppliers sell special stencil paper, traditionally made from oiled manilla. You can now use materials such as vinyl or clear acetate, or newspaper if spraying on paint. For difficult shapes and surfaces you can use masking tape or low tack soft peel masking film to make a form of stencil.

Before you start, choose your design. You may wish to take a motif from a piece of fabric, a greetings card, or painting, and turn it into a stencil.

The methods are as follows:

1. Trace the design on paper and then put it onto the stencil paper by placing a piece of carbon paper, face down, between the original design and the stencil paper. Go over the design pressing hard with a pen, then draw over the marks left by the carbon paper with a waterproof black felt tip.

2. Photocopy the design and stick it onto stencil paper or card and then cut out the design.

3. Photocopy the design, stick the acetate over it and then cut out. If you wish to draw on acetate use a rapidograph.

Cutting a Stencil

1. Tape the stencil paper or acetate with the design drawn onto it, onto a flat cutting board made of chipboard, plywood or blockwood.
2. Leave a good 2cm border round the edge of the stencil paper for strength.
3. Using the tip of the blade of a craft knife, Stanley knife or ideally a scalpel, cut round the inked outlines using a firm fluent movement.
   TIP: It is easier to move the paper and keep the knife still on curved surfaces.
4. If your design consists of two or more stencils, mark where they join with registration marks: for example, a cross or hole in each corner of the stencil paper which can be dotted with a pencil or tailors' chalk to show the position of the first stencil when you come to print the next part of the design. Alternatively a small registration mark can be cut in the stencil paper which can then be aligned, but take care not to paint over this mark.

How to align Stencils

If you are stencilling a repeat design, work out before you start, how many repeats fit into the article you are stencilling by measuring the width of the cloth and dividing this by the width of the design.

1. Measure the distance you want between repeats, put the stencil in the correct place and mark through the registration holes with a pencil, or tailors' chalk.
2. Place the stencil in its next position taking care to align with registration marks and repeat.
3. If you are using a second stencil make sure that it fits between or over the first one. Follow steps 1 and 2 before beginning to print.
4. Before printing a second stencil let the colour from the first dry completely.

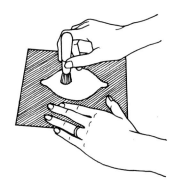

A FIRST STENCIL PROJECT ON A SMALL PIECE OF FABRIC

Method

1. Fix the fabric to the stencilling board with drawing pins or tape.
2. Fix the stencil to the fabric with masking tape.
3. For a design using more than one stencil there will be registration marks. Mark these with a 'Magic' pen, pencil or tailors' chalk.
4. Select the colours. Put only small amounts onto a saucer or plate. You need plenty of space on your saucer for mixing colours and for removing excess dye from your stencilling brush.
5. Choose a dry brush — small ones for small details and larger ones for larger shapes. Note: Never use a wet brush when stencilling as this causes the design to bleed.
6. Hold your brush in an upright position. Dip it into the dye. Remove the excess as you only want a little paint on the brush.
7. Hold the stencil down with one hand and keep the stencil brush vertical in the other. Stamp the dye onto the cloth with an up-and-down motion.
8. Allow the paint to dry thoroughly before removing the stencil.
9. Fix the cloth by ironing. The registration marks will wash out.

Materials

Insulation board on which to pin your fabric
Drawing pins or tape
Masking tape
Magic pen — one which will wash out, or soft pencil, or tailor's chalk
Stencil
Stencil brush — these are stubby, hard bristled brushes with flat ends
Fabric paint

Tips

1. For a shaded effect start with the palest shade you want.
2. For a well-blended effect, cover the entire shape with the pale colour. Then put a darker colour on the brush and continue stamping.
3. If you want a very dark area of colour, do not cover the area with the very pale shade. Instead do the pale area first and then the dark area. Stamp about where the two areas meet in order to blend them.

MARBLING

Marbling is one of the simplest and most effective ways of decorating a surface with a pattern. It is called marbling for obvious reasons as the end result often resembles the wavy and veined patterns present in marble.

Marbling is the creation of designs or patterns on the surface of water which are then transferred to other surfaces. The process relies on the fact that oil and water do not mix and the earliest known method was to float oil colours on water.

It is thought to have its origins in Turkey. At one time marbled paper was smuggled into this country from Holland wrapped around parcels of toys, thus escaping the import duty. On arrival it was flattened and sold to book binders to use as end papers.

Method

1. If you are making a gelatine size do this first by dissolving one dessertspoonful of gelatine in one pint of water (follow maker's instructions for mixing) and use at room temperature. If not fill your container ¾ full of water.
2. Lay newspaper on the floor to place the objects on whilst they dry.
3. Thin your colours with white spirit so that they are runny.
4. Drop your colour in small amounts onto the container of water. If the colour sinks to the bottom it needs thinning with more white spirit or turpentine substitute.
5. Swirl the pattern around with a stick or pencil.
6. Put on the rubber gloves. When marbling tiles, grip them in your hand, then place them glazed side down on the surface of the water and lift up. Leave to dry.
7. Anything which has a flat surface (paper or china, etc.) may be laid on the surface of the water to collect the paint. Other objects need to be completely submerged and will collect the colour as they pass through it.
8. Marble candles by holding their wicks and immersing the rest in water.
9. When marbling a jar or bottle, bend a wire coat hanger to fit

Materials

1. *A large container such as a square washing up bowl, photographic dish, roasting pan or kitchen sink.*
2. *Solvent or oil based paints. The Pebeo Ceramic à Froid and Couleurs Vitrails paints are ideal as are any oil-based paints.*
   NOTE: If you wish to print with water-based paints a size must be made from Carrageen Moss (Irish Seaweed). Size is a penetrating liquid of gluey consistency which prepares a surface for further coverage — usually canvas for oil paints, etc. The fabric or paper you are printing on has to be treated with a mordant, or fixative.

inside as a handle.

10. Ceramic and glass objects can be coated with varnish to protect them. This does not apply to candles due to the flammable nature of the varnish — they should be dipped in melted wax.

3. White spirit.
4. Instrument for stirring the paint, or the back of an old paint brush.
5. A pair of rubber gloves.
6. Some jam jars, lids, saucers for mixing colours.
7. Old newspaper.
8. (Optional) Packet of powdered gelatine, which thickens the water slightly and gives more control over the patterns. It was not used in the marbled objects in the book.

BLOCK PRINTING

Block printing is the application of colour onto one, usually embossed, surface and then pressing the colour onto another flat surface. Wooden and metal blocks, often with intricate patterns, have been used for centuries in the Indian textile industry and are still used today.

Many hard fruits and vegetables — onions, apples, pears, peppers, carrots and parsnips — when cut in half have in-built patterns that can be used for printing.

The vegetable most commonly associated with printing is the potato, cheap and easily available. Your design is not limited to the size of the potato as a design can be built up by repeating one motif several times or by using different motifs. Used corks from wine bottles can also be carved for use as interestingly textured printing blocks.

Making a Potato Print

1. Wash, peel and cut the potato in half. Make sure you have a flat surface for printing.
2. Designs can be cut in several ways. The round shape of the

Marbling a ceramic tile.

existing potato can be used as it stands. Or you can draw a design on it in felt tip and cut the potato around it away so that the design stands out. Or you can cut the design away so that the surround stands proud.

NOTE: The projecting part of the design is the bit which will print.

3. Using a small vegetable knife cut away any excess potato. The remaining design stands proud of the rest of the potato.

4. On a piece of newspaper dab off any surplus starch.

5. Apply the fabric paint (Setacolor or a fabric paint of a similar consistency) using a paint brush. The paint can be diluted with water. Cover the raised surface of the block with colour and press it down firmly but gently onto the surface you are to print. It is a good idea to test the paint first on a piece of paper.

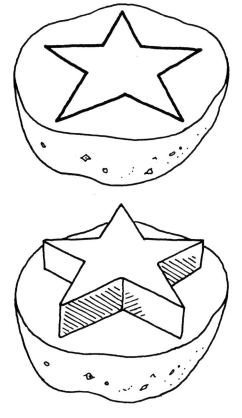

Potato Prints.

6. Print a test piece on material if you are doing fabric painting, on wood if you are printing on wood. Adjust the amount of colour you put on the potato according to the result you achieve.

If you wish the repeat to be even in colour the block will need recolouring between each print.

If you wish the colour to be graded in its intensity print without repainting the block with colour.

It is a good idea to use a different potato for each colour as potatoes are absorbent and a first colour is likely to show through a second one.

Tips

1. You will have to make new blocks each day as potatoes go soft if left overnight.
2. For the best results lay the material to be printed on a padded surface. This can be made with layers of newspaper or an old blanket or sheet. This provides the necessary resistance and gives an even coverage.

PAINTING ON WALLS

A bare white wall may be daunting to begin with, but as with most of the projects in this book it can be as easy or as complicated as you wish to make it.

Some Simple Ideas

1. Soft tack masking tape, the sort that is easily removed, is great for masking off areas and making geometric patterns. Use it to make borders of colour round the edge of a dado rail, or round a doorway.
2. Make triangular shapes round the edge of a bath.
3. Paint a cascade of flowers and leaves from a wall light (photo p. 122). These were drawn freehand in pencil and then painted in artist' oils — these are waterproof and allow the wall to be washed. Copy the design from the template on p. 123 and paint in the same way, using acrylic or oil based paints.

Painting on walls.

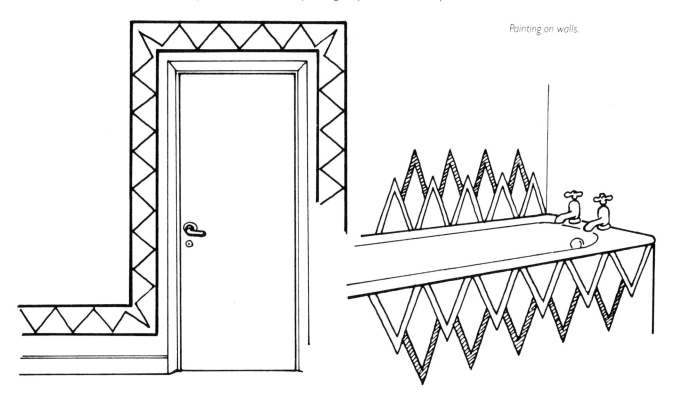

Floral wall painting.

4. A child's nursery can be made pretty with a very simple device of balloons cut out of coloured paper and then joined together by painting on ribbons and bows. The joy of using paper is you can cut out shapes, and 'blue tack' them into place to see if they look right before making the final decision. Connecting ribbons can be drawn in pencil before being painted in using fluid acrylic paint.

5. Cut out other paper shapes for children's rooms such as a jungle with monkeys and parrots.

Either use the cut paper shapes to draw round and then colour in with paint. Or paint on the paper and then stick it down with wallpaper paste when you are happy with the result.

DESIGN
DIRECTORY

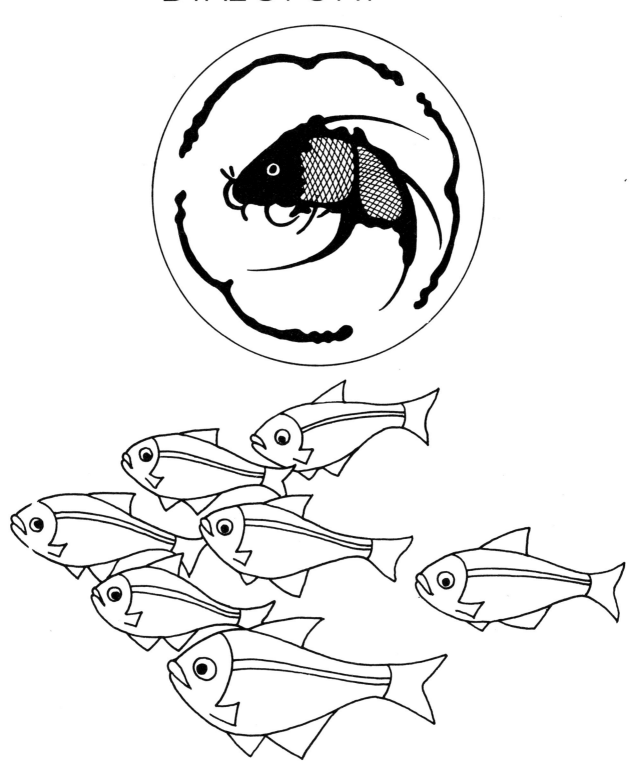

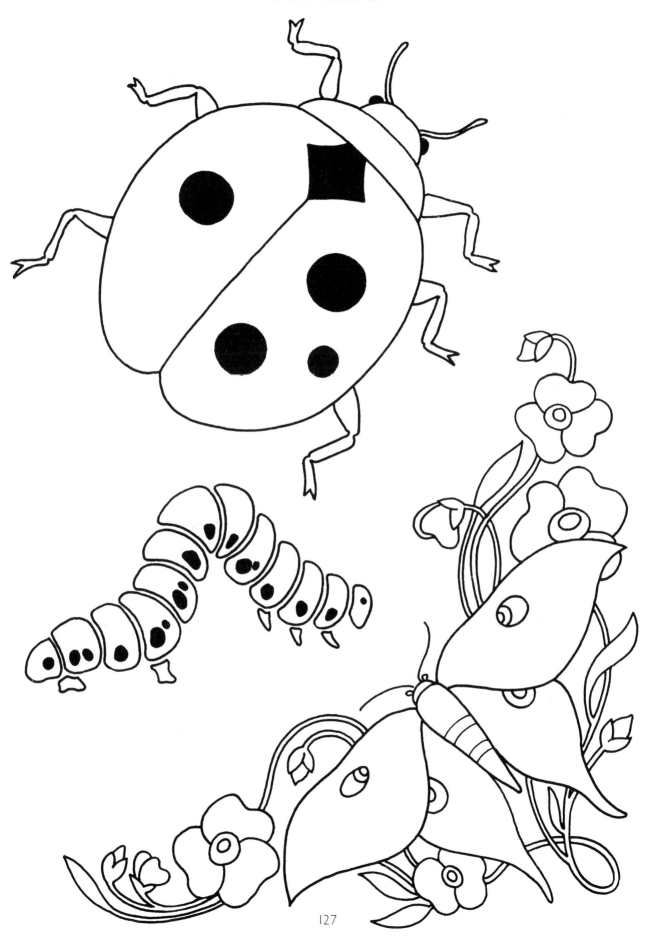

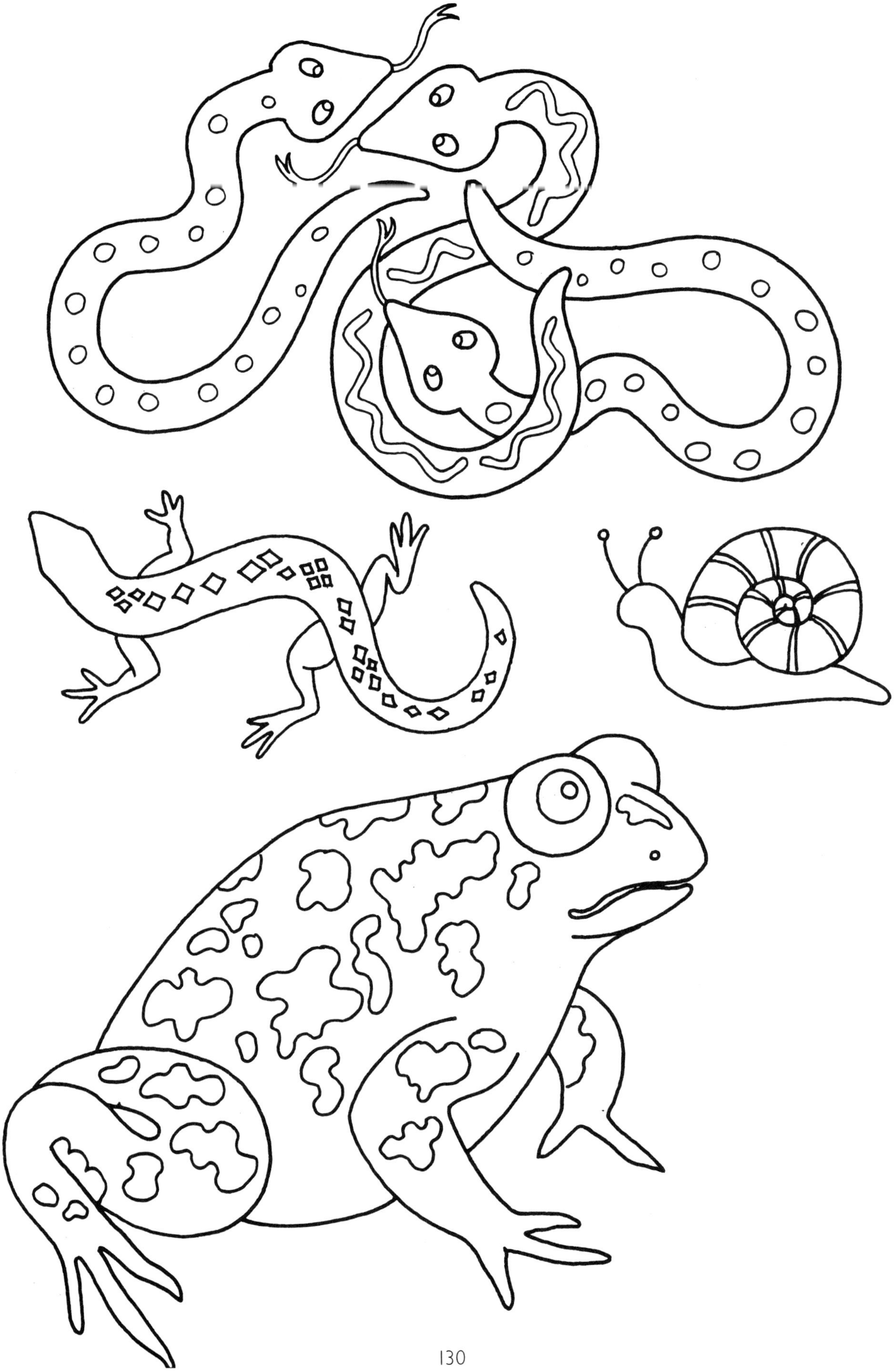

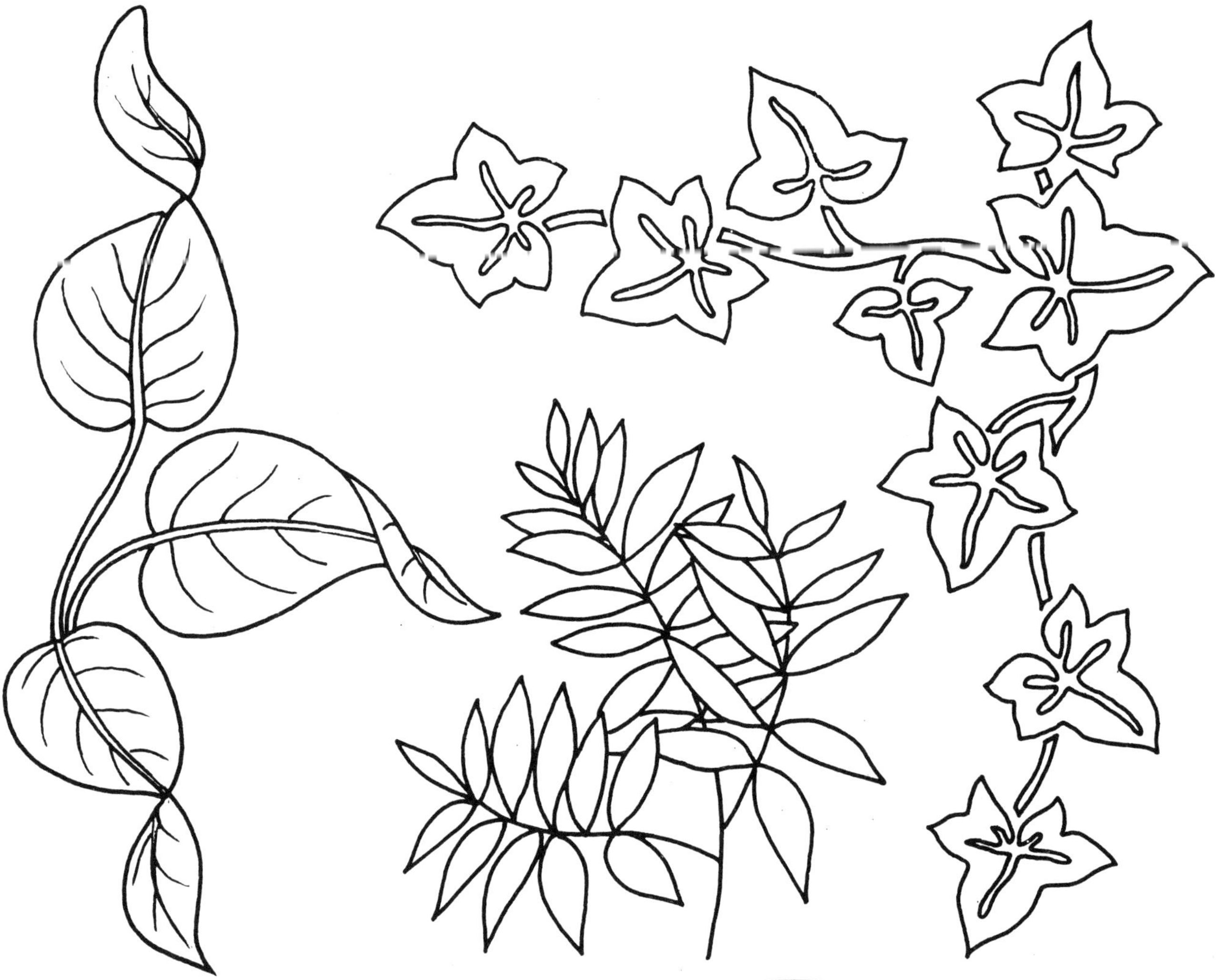

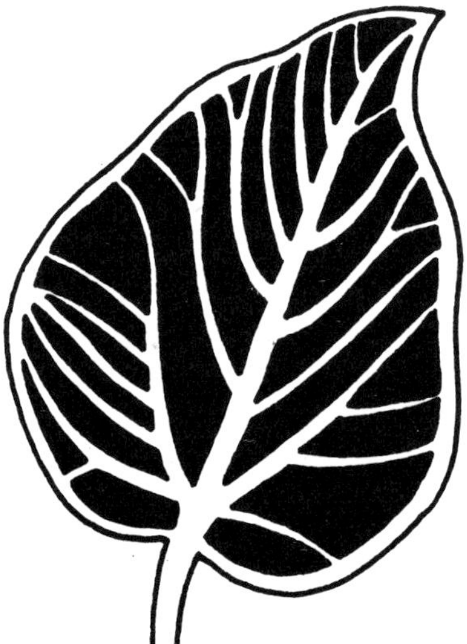

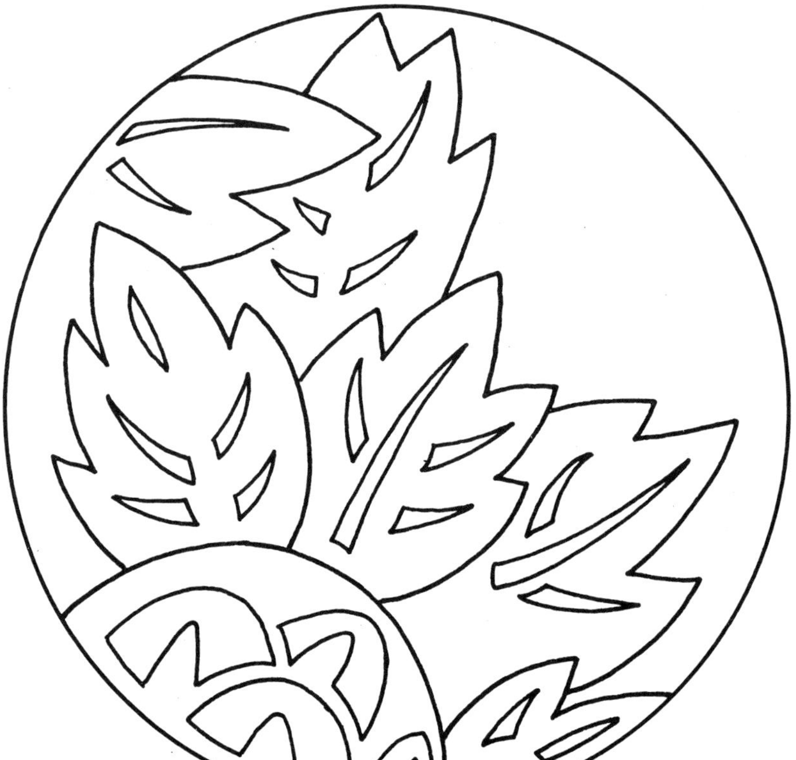

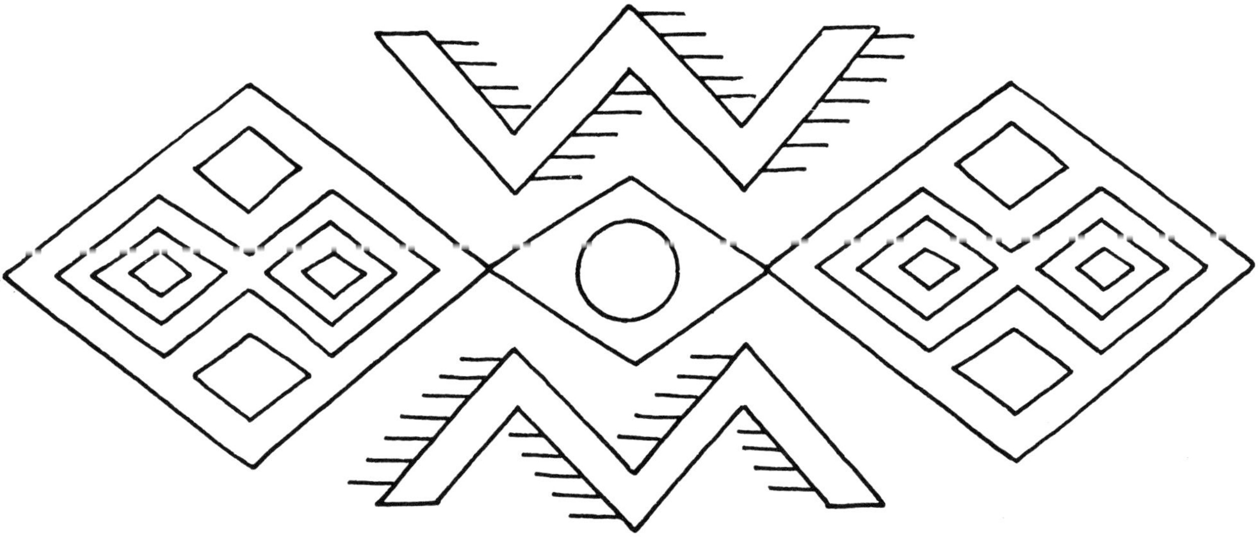

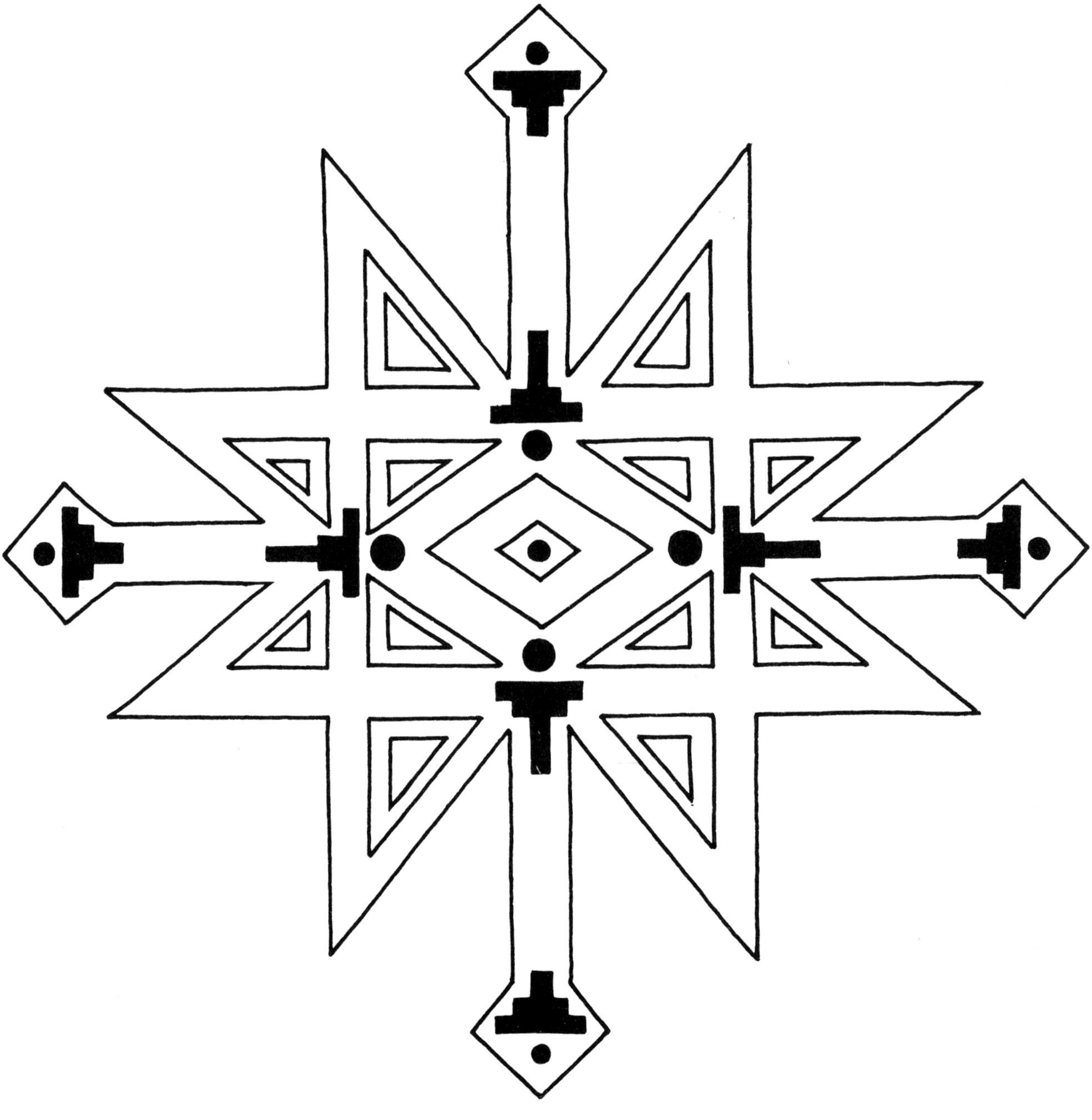

PRODUCTS USED IN THIS BOOK

The following Pebeo products pass the AFNOR STANDARD S51204 and are considered safe. Most products are stocked in 45ml and 250ml bottles although larger quantities are available.

Setacolor

An all-fabric paint available in 44 colours, for painting, dyeing, spraying and printing cottons, polyesters, silks, etc. SETACOLOR can be mixed together and diluted with water and fixed or 'heat set' to the fabric by ironing. The paints are available in four different finishes — opaque, transparent, pearlized and fluorescent, according to the weight and nature of the fabric used.

Setaskrib

Fabric felt tip pens for most fabrics in 12 colours. Refill bottles and new felt tips available. Fix colour to fabric by ironing.

Pebeo Star

All-surface glitter paint in 10 colours. It is washable once fixed to fabric by ironing.

Set Air

Concentrated textile colours for use with an air brush.

Orient Express

Concentrate dye for silk and wool in 20 intermixable colours. Water diluteable, it can be fixed by using a special fixative or steam fixing.

Liquid Fixative

Fixative solution for Orient Express. Dilute with water (30ml fixative to 1 litre of cold water). Fix silk for five minutes after waiting at least 48 hours and rinse immediately in cold water.

Gutta

Liquid, gum-like solution in solvent base for outlining on silk or cotton. Available in neutral, gold, silver or black (clear, water-based guttaq is also available).

Ceramic a Froid

High gloss, opaque enamel for most surfaces in 22 intermixable colours. Cold setting, it can be thinned and cleaned out of brushes with white spirit.

Ceramic a l'Eau

Water based ceramic paints in 10 colours. Wait 24 hours after using and bake ceramic in a low temperature domestic oven for half an hour.

Couleurs Vitrails

Transparent paint in 10 colours (some of which can be mixed) for most surfaces particularly glass, acetate, aluminium and wood. Can also be added to clear solvent based gutta for coloured gutta.

Vitrail a l'Eau

Water based glass paint in nine colours.

Cerne Relief Vitrail

Acrylic/water based imitation lead relief in a tube (NON TOXIC).

Light Deco

Liquid, matt acrylic paint in 21 colours giving a dense coverage. Water-based, but waterproof once dry. For all surfaces, particularly wood and plaster. It is suitable for external use.

Vernis a la Cire

Vernis a la Cire is a satin, wax like varnish which sinks in and *very* slightly darkens wood. Being water and alcohol resistant, it is very suitable for protecting painted wooden kitchen objects where a high gloss finish is NOT desired. Repeated layers of Vernis a la Cire will render the object heatproof making it suitable for pot stands, etc. Wash brushes in white spirit.

Vernis a Patiner

Vernis a Patiner is an extremely high gloss, slow drying varnish which is applied with a brush. Repeated layers will give a lacquered look and though you should sand your object with glasspaper between each layer, it is not strictly necessary. Wash brushes in white spirit. Pebeo Light Deco is a suitable paint for use under this varnish but repeated layers of Ceramic a Froid and Vernis a Patiner will build up an attractive three dimensional lacquered look. The layers of varnish can take a couple of days to be *completely* dry. Be patient!

Vernis a Craqueler

Vernis a Craqueler is a crackling varnish which is generally applied with a brush on top of Vernis a Patiner (for method see separate instructions on p. 66). As the name implies, the varnish gives the decorated object an old, crazed look. China decorated with Ceramic a Froid (high gloss paint) can also be 'crackled' by brushing Vernis a Craqueler directly on top of the Ceramic a Froid when it is 'just dry to the touch'. The crackles appear 15-20 minutes later. The china object should then be given a final protective varnish using Crystal Varnish or Couverte Brillante.

Objects to be Primed

Occasionally you will find that the paint you are using for decoration will 'sink in' to the object.

Wood & Plaster
Wood can be primed with a 50%-50% mixture of Vernis a la Cire and white spirit. This should be evenly brushed on the wood and left to dry. This also preserves the natural colour of the wood. Decorate the object with Light Deco. Alternatively, Sous Couche Incolore, a water based acrylic primer, can be used as a wood primer when using Couleurs Vitrails or Ceramic a Froid. Sous Couche Incolore is of a much thicker consistency and is ideal for priming absorbent plaster casts.

For a complete up-to-date list of all the materials used in the book, contact:

ARTEMIS PRODUCTS LTD
684 MITCHAM ROAD
CROYDON CR9 3AB

Telephone: 01-684 1330

Pebeo of America
P O Box 373
Williston
VT 05495
Tel. 802 658 9516

Francheville
74 Lygon Street
East Brunswick
Victoria 3057
Tel. 419 89 95